Stan: An American Story

D1202613

A few words from my friends:

Stan Gober—I'm not sure, but I think he bought me a drink . . . once!

I used to enjoy going to Stan's and playing pool, before he put the stage and dance floor in. I managed to win my share and the bartenders loved it because they discovered "tipping" was not a city in China. Hated to see that pool table go, but that's progress.

I also enjoyed introducing the King Buzzard, but Stan never did convince me to do that crazy buzzard dance.

KEN VENTURI
Golfing Legend—1964 U.S. Open Champion

Stan Gober, what a character! Americana at its best. I always know at Stan's I will have a good time and meet a lot of interesting people. Stan indeed is a great American—despite *thinking* he's a Democrat.

JOHN A. BOEHNER
Congressman, Ohio

Stan is my favorite high-tech redneck—a codgy old guy with mass appeal.

At Stan's you have millionaires pretending to be bikers, boaters pretending to be boaters and regular people trying to be not regular. And everybody gets along. It all works because of the special atmosphere that only Stan could create.

One reason I live on Marco is because of Stan's.

WES BATES
Owner of Stanley Steemer Carpet Cleaners
Proud Resident of Marco Island

Stan Gober is a special American treasure. He personifies what is good about the American spirit through his charitable endeavors and his willingness to help people, he has established himself as one of the most recognizable faces in Southwest Florida.

His love and talent for music add to the charm that is Stan Gober.

Based in Nashville, Tennessee, I have had the opportunity to know Stan for over 15 years. During that time, we have had the opportunity to entertain him several times during his stops in Music City. Whether he is attending showcases up here, participating in the CMA Music Festival (formerly known as Fan Fair) or just going out to dinner, he always exudes the same enthusiasm and energy that he does when he is on stage in Goodland, Florida.

He is indeed a special person and one whose friendship Terri and I and our family cherish.

He is an American treasure we feel lucky to have discovered.

JEFF AND TERRI WALKER
President, AristoMedia/Marco Productions

What do I have to say about Stan? Nobody has ever met Stan who doesn't love him instantly! But the big puzzle for me has been . . . how does he ever fit that huge, wonderful heart into his regular size body? Guess I'll never figure that one out. The man reaches out to anyone in distress, anyone who needs help, anyone who is hurting, and never looks for a return. Stan is truly a friend to everyone he meets.

DONNA FIALA
Collier County Commissioner

Having known Stan for over 30 years, he is one of the most generous persons you'll encounter.

His talent as an entertainer and host are remarkable, but Stan does have problems with his speech and vocabulary on occasion.

I can recall a time during the Marco Film Festival Party at Stan's Idle Hour, I was doing a television interview with Stan regarding the appearance of Ben Gazzara. There was just no way Stan could pronounce Gazzara. After at least 6 takes, I gave up and included Gazzara's name in the question so Stan wouldn't have to say it.

Stan has had several health problems over the years, which he's been able to overcome. His latest is back pain which will eventually require surgery. While discussing this with friends recently, Stan kept referring to the fact he was seeing a UROLOGIST. I finally was able to get Stan's attention and inform him if he was going to undergo back surgery, I hoped he meant to say he was seeing a NEUROLOGIST.

Barbara and I cannot say enough about Stan, a genuine, caring and gracious person, a true friend always.

JOE AND BARBARA KLIMAS
Local radio and television sportscaster and his wife

What can I say about Stan? What an amazing fellow! His scraggly appearance is just a front to relax all who meet him and to ensure we trust him, enjoy ourselves and appreciate the fact that we live in the greatest country on earth. Stan is, in fact, the epitome of America. His down-home humor, his indomitable patriotism, his generous heart and his powerful ability to make us all appreciate the gifts God has given us make him a blessing to people around the world. For you see, people do come from everywhere . . . by car, by boat, by motorcycle and by plane . . . just to experience the gift to us all that is our beloved Stan.

And when the strains of Sandi Patty singing "The Star Spangled Banner" roll across the precious island of Goodland, Florida . . . when there is not a dry eye in the place or a sound among the crowd, you know that Stan was put on this earth to make us all better!

God bless you, Stan, for all that you do and all that you are! We are truly better people because we are your friends!

DONNA HAZLE GLANZMAN
2003 Mrs. All American
Columbus, Ohio and Marco Island, FL

I first met Stan in 1973. On fishing junkets with other snow birds from Minnesota we became hooked on the Stan experience. Little did I know at that time that Stan Gober would become a legend—an extraordinarily ordinary person.

There is simply no place on earth like Stan's on a Sunday afternoon. It's a redneck Woodstock that is easily enjoyed by Manhattan socialites. The band plays. Stan sings and tells jokes. The crowd enjoys grilled hamburgers, fried grouper and cold beer. You haven't lived until you have experienced the unique atmosphere that Stan creates.

He is a genuine friend to all persons he meets and has no limit to hosting fund-raising events.

For his success, Stan gives credit to Jesus whom he confirms, "Leads him every step of the way."

CINDY ANDERSON
Retired Educator/Volunteer

We have been privileged to know Stan Gober for twenty years. Stan has a great personality, the type of person people like immediately when they meet him. Stan is a born entertainer with musical talent. He has written some really fun songs and sings them on stage at his "Stan's Idle Hour Restaurant"; songs like "Yankee Dollar," "What Kind of Fish Is That" and his classic "The Buzzard Lope." He loves to tell jokes and he's good at that. The other side of his personality is a man of faith, a family man and a real American patriot.

BOB & PAT FLAGG
Retired Police Commissioner,
St. Louis County (Missouri) Police Department

I first met Stan 17–18 years ago and we became friends immediately. We are much alike. I enjoy making people happy at our hotel on the Chesapeake Bay in Tilghman, Maryland and Stan also enjoys making people happy. We came to his place kind of by accident. We went fishing with his son Russ years ago and when we got back, heard all of this country western music being played. We looked up and saw such a good time going on we decided to go back to the house and shower and then go back and listen to it ourselves.

Stan is a multi-talented person and tells a great joke! Everyone can tell a joke but not everyone can tell it with a great delivery. Stan tells it like that. He's just magnificent. He also has that southern accent that adds to his joke telling. He has such a unique ability for story telling that he just holds the attention of the audience to the point where they are almost in a hypnotic state. Not only is he a great joke teller but also a very talented singer. He is the total package.

Stan's been coming up to our establishment in Maryland every year. He has created quite a following for himself. People always call to find out when he will be here as it is the highlight of the summer for some of these people. He makes a long weekend of it and people flock in to see him. His brand of humor isn't always readily available around here.

In closing, Stan is just a unique sort of person. Finding a talented performer is always something of a bonus. To have that same person become someone you admire, have a lot in common with, and most of all call a friend, is truly the icing on the cake.

CAPT. BUDDY HARRISON III
Harrison's Chesapeake House & Sport Fishing
Tilghman, Maryland

My wife Kathy and I have helped Stan with many benefits over the past eleven years including our 11th Hospice of Naples benefit held on December 10, 2005. Which reminds me of the time Stan almost gave me a heart attack.

I talked Comcast TV into televising the Hospice benefit live from 12 p.m. to 6 p.m. at a reduced cost. Comcast told me that we would have to follow a strict schedule, minute by minute. Never having done this before I began finding out how long each song lasted, the time all the performers would arrive and how long they would perform. In addition I had to find out the length of time each commercial would take. It took me about 3 weeks with many changes. I finally got it approved by Comcast.

On the morning of the benefit around 10:30 I gave Stan his copy and he said, "What the hell is this?" I told him the TV crew needed it because we were live, and that was how we had to do it so we would not look like we didn't know what we were doing. We had to keep it moving on time.

Stan said "Ah hell, I can't do that. We're just going up there and do our thing like always." And he tossed my schedule away. I thought I was going to die. About 30 minutes later I saw Stan had picked it up and was reading it. He told me it looked good and we would use it. He carried it in his hand the whole afternoon even on live TV.

Stan has raised hundreds of thousands of dollars for a lot of good organizations that help a lot of local people in need. We know he will continue to help people and when he calls, Kathy and I will be there.

LARRY P. SCHEETZ & KATHLEEN K. HUGHES
Accu-Care Nursing Service, Inc

I met Stan in 1988 when he invited me to share a meal of fried cat fish, hush puppies, black eyed peas and greens on the ever popular deck at Stan's in Goodland. Discovering we both enjoyed the finer tastes in life, we became instant friends.

While many people appreciate Stan for his humor and ability to entertain, my thoughts are of his love of life and the people from all phases of life he comes into contact with. I value our conversations about life's lessons encountered in the hospitality business. I continue to value our friendship.

Did you know his mother actually planned to name him Star, but the *r* turned out like an *n*?

STAN BRUNS
Former General Manager,
Marco Island Marriott Resort and Golf Club

Stan is a 'can do' man—a man of action! He knows a good idea when he hears one and he knows how to act on it and get things done. If you ask him to lend a hand to help people in need he's with you all the way, regardless of whether the help is for someone in Goodland, families in the Naples area, or survivors of international disasters.

Through his sponsorship of 'Celebration of Life' and participation as Grand Marshal in the Goodland boat parade, he has helped Goodland raise hundreds of thousands of dollars for Hospice of Naples, and that's just one charity for which he regularly hosts fund-raising events.

By sponsoring many annual fund-raising events and by facing his own adversities with courage and determination he is an inspiration to the community and all who know him.

ELAINE RITCHIE
A friend and neighbor
Founder of the Mardi Gras Goodland Boat Parade

Integrity, Heart and Humor. Those are the characteristics that come to mind when I think of Stan Gober. I first met Stan in the early 80s when my late husband Terry and I walked into the bar although it was closed. They were having a private family party. But Stan invited us in and made us feel at home.

Two of the fund-raising events that come to mind are the Goodland Boat Parade in February and Celebration of Life in December to benefit Hospice. Stan will help anyone at any time. He is a true humanitarian.

KITTY NOOM & JOE PATAVA
Stan's close friends from Traverse City, Michigan

My wife Susan and I would never dream of a trip to Florida without many Sundays spent at Stan's! It is indeed a unique experience!! Besides enjoying Stan, his family, music and of course his jokes we always see friends, old and new. We even run into Bob Lurtzima, retired defensive tackle with the Minnesota Vikings who played across from me during the glory years (ours)—Among the memories I will cherish forever are: doing the Buzzard Lope Dance and hardly able to get up afterward . . . The sight of me with my legs in the air must be a vision to behold! But, the best part of a wonderful day is ending the show on the stage singing "God Bless America" with Stan leading the crowd. He is a super human being with so much love for people and his country. We are very blessed to know him. . . .

FUZZY AND SUE THURSTON
Baltimore Colts 1958
Green Bay Packers 1961–1968 (the Lombardi glory years)
Five championships including first two Super Bowls

And finally the following appeared in the Marco Island Eagle on May 28, 1997:

Man of the Year Typifies "Service before Self"

Marco Island Sunrise Rotary president-elect, Dr. Peter Nowosielski, has paid tribute to the club's Man of the Year, Stan Gober.

"He has been involved, through a lifetime of commitment to helping others," said Dr. Nowosielski. "He fits Rotary's image of service before self."

Dr. Nowosielski said other services rendered by Gober, the popular entertainer and proprietor of Stan's Idle Hour Restaurant on Goodland, included donating his services to the club's successful "Gift of Life" program, American Cancer Society, Blind of Naples, Hospice, Make a Wish Foundation, Goodland Scholarship Fund via Village Productions, Mullet Festival, helping the local fire department and "numerous personal benefits for individuals with a myriad of serious illnesses and malignancies.

"He doesn't know how to say no. Part of his philosophy is stated simply: 'I have Jesus Christ in my heart. Every day I wake and ask for His help through the day. Faith got me here,'" said Dr. Nowosielski, recalling Gober's words.

Gober, continued Dr. Nowosielski, adhered to the drug-free philosophy in both his own life and that of his business, and also warned against the abuse of alcohol with the philosophy: "If you can't handle it, don't use it."

Dr. Nowosielski concluded that Gober was a perfect choice for Marco Island's Sunrise Rotary Club's Man of the Year.

"Would that the world shared and practiced his philosophy," he said.

Stan
An American Story

Stan Gober

KELLER PUBLISHING

ISBN-13: 978-0-9674128-6-3
ISBN-10: 0-9674128-6-2

Designed and composed
by Hobblebush Books,
Brookline, New Hampshire
Printed in the United States of America

Published by

KELLER PUBLISHING
590 Fieldstone Drive
Marco Island, Florida 34145

800-631-1952
KellerPublishing.com

I DEDICATE THIS BOOK TO:

My mother
Bertie

My wife
Faye

My children
Rebecca

Russ

Jay

Steve

My grandchildren
Nicole

Colin

David

Crystal

Michael

Dylan

Ryan

Jared

Zachary

Bethany

Jacob

My Great-grandchildren
Chelsea
Robert

CONTENTS

ACKNOWLEDGMENTS

I'd like to mention how I met Wade Keller. A few months ago, over at the Marco Inn, I was asked to make a little talk about why I moved to Goodland and Marco Island. It was for the Historical Society. There were four speakers, and I was the last one. Of course, I just told the story of why I moved over here and how.

After it was all over, Wade stepped up and introduced himself to me, and said he would like to do my autobiography. And I said, "You mean write a book?"

And he said, "Ya!"

I said, "I don't know man, why would you want to do that?"

He said, "Well, I think it's a story here. People will read your story and at times they will laugh and at times they will cry. That's a powerful story."

Y'know, I've been asked by people before why I didn't write a book and I always told them, "I can't write. I can't hardly read, much less write. There's no way I could do that!" And they'd say, "Well, get somebody to write it for ya!"

So Wade stepped up and he said he'd like to do that. He said, "You just tell it to me, I'll write it." So that's what we did. And this is it and I hope you like it. I want to thank him very much for that. I also want to thank Wade's wife, Sue, for taking some pictures and being so supportive in the whole thing here.

I'd also like to thank you, reading this book right now. I just hope you enjoy it.

And while I'm in the "Thank You" mode here I'd like to thank some people for the privilege of singing with them over the years. I just want to thank all those who have helped me along the way.

Bobby Gideon, over at the Olde Marco Inn, is a great entertainer and a great piano player. He always invited me to sing when I was over there on Marco, and I've sang with him a lot of times for his audience.

Then there was Johnny Angel, I sang with him a lot all around.

Alan Bogden played the piano, and I used to sing with him and Jackie Lee.

Mitch Peters is a great piano player who entertained at the Hilton. I sang with him a lot.

Anywhere I went that somebody was playing, I could ask them or sometimes they would ask me to sing with them. So I've had that kind of good rapport on Marco, which has been good for me. By going out like that around to those places it actually helped us get some folks going to our place too. It allowed me to invite people. I'd ask them if I could say something about Stan's and they'd always say "yeah."

Bob Snyder has played at my place. He's on a couple of my songs, "Yankee Dollar" and "Stuck on a Sandbar." I sang with him a lot at different places on the beach, at the Marriott, with his band over at the Marco Inn or on the boat, the *Rosie O'Shea*.

Also, I want to mention my good friends, Jeff and Terri Walker, in Nashville. They're in the entertainment business. His wife was a great singer, had a CD out and they met, they got married and she gave it up. She'd toured all over Europe and Canada. One great singer.

He's in the publicity business of the great big country stars in Nashville. He treats me just beautiful when I go up there. We go backstage at the Grand Ole Opry. We been on a train out of Nashville goin' through the hills with cocktails and music, with singers that they're promoting, and puttin' on a show. You know they're just wonderful people. I've been to "FanFair" with them three times, and they always get me on stage with the singers, and they just treat me wonderful.

They have two houses in Goodland. In fact, they're building two brand new houses in Goodland now. And this is where they come for their vacation. Jeff is the son of Bill Walker, who was the music director for the Statler Brothers and their TV show for all those years. He is a piano player, and he's a great arranger of music. He's arranged many, many sessions for the big country singers in Nashville.

On Christmas about four years ago, Jeff and Terri gave me a picture of Bing Crosby with his signature. Then on another Christmas, they gave me a little Santa Claus of the Bing singing "White Christmas." So you know, they know how I feel about entertainment and stuff.

Of course, I want to thank Ray Nesbit and Roger Raymond of the Morningstar Show Band. I sang with them a lot of times. We had the occasion one time to do New Year's Eve at the Marriott in the main ballroom. They were playing the Buzzard Song, and we were all dressed up in tuxedos and laid down on the floor and did the Buzzard Dance. That was a good time!

I'd like to thank Ray Young, who used to produce the Four Tops. He lives on Marco. Back in those days, he had the job of bringing entertainment to the Marco Beach Hotel on the holidays. He brought the Four Tops, Four Impressions, Fifth Dimension, the Ink Spots, and a few others. We would always go there to do celebrations because we weren't doing the New Year's Eve entertainment at that time.

Ray would bring all these bands to my Sunday Show. I would introduce them from my stage, then everybody would have a fit over these guys and everything. In fact, the Four Impressions got on stage and sang the Buzzard Song with me! We had a good time.

I want to thank the Mackle brothers. They had great entertainment when they owned Marco Beach Hotel. I met The Fifth Dimension there. That was a highlight to me. Then I corresponded with them for about three years. They all lived in Beverly Hills, California. That was fun times.

The only "big shot" who ever sang at my place, the only really well-known singer that ever sang at my place was Tracy Lawrence. He did an hour show one time on my stage, through Jim Turner, the man who was the CEO of the Stetson Hat Company. He moved his office from New York to Naples, and he had Tracy Lawrence come in one night after we'd done the show all day. He brought 400 people from all around the world on a big boat out of Marco. I entertained them with the band, then Tracy come on and sang.

Tracy Lawrence was under contract with the Stetson hat people. Mr. Turner bought all of my help a Stetson. He had me pick one out too. Oh, man, beautiful hat. I still have it.

Thanks to John Stevens, a young country singer from Ohio who was one of the first performers at Stan's. He filled in when Kevin Thomas took off to Nashville.

I want to thank Willie Nelson. We were born the same day, but I'm seven years older than him. I met him about four times although we've never really got together. I've got a picture of him on his bus, and I've been to his shows.

Thank you to A.B. Martin for helping me start the Mullet Festival. A.B. Martin was the one that came up with the idea. He's a roofer, owns his own business, finance company, and he used to be my neighbor here.

I want to thank Kevin Thomas, especially for rewriting the Gilligan's Island theme:

Just sit right back, and you'll hear a tale / The tale of a fateful trip / That started in Alabama / And brought us one more hick!

That's how he always used to introduce me. That just tickled me. Kevin made the arrangements for my first ten songs. He's just a great talent. We've been entertaining together for almost 20 years.

I have to say a special thanks to Anna Yamonis, now Mrs. John Carter. I also want to thank Lynn, my present girlfriend, who's been great to me. We've been together 14 years this January 2006.

I got a lotta people to thank for just supportin' what we do.

I really want to thank especially the people who come to my place faithfully. They just say it's a place to come on Sunday.

In fact, Merle Allen a guitar player and singer, named his song "Stan's on Sunday" after us, and we sing it every Sunday. Merle is a great entertainer and a great guy who has always asked me to sing wherever he plays.

Bill Hughes, I have to thank him for doing the video of the things that we've done. In fact, I think I'm on the video for the Historical Society that he made up. He and his wife are entertainers and they go all around entertaining. They're really great entertainers too. Bill is the one who makes my CDs for me.

I want to say thank you to my family. My kids work. They've been there with me to make the place go. Russ, Steve and Jay. Jay moved to North Carolina. We've only been separated for a few years. I used to get them to do all kind of things, so they were all around, and that's one reason we made it.

I've been blessed because I'm doing what I like to do, and I actually make a living doing it. I don't think you can do any better than that. I'm entertaining and getting paid and running a restaurant and getting paid. I'm doing what I want to do, and the Lord directed me to do this.

That's what I'm thankful for because I know that's the truth.

Stan: An American Story

≈ 1 ≈

YOU DON'T CATCH THE SNOOK—
THE SNOOK CATCHES YOU

I always say you don't catch the snook, the snook catches you because once you catch it, you're hooked. In 1958 working for the phone company in Miami—there wasn't but one then—I was always in the top three for production. I was one hard-working son of a gun.

One Sunday afternoon, my wife, Faye, and our first son, Russell, were at home when our new neighbor, who had recently moved down from Georgia, pulled into our driveway. As he pulled in, you could see that his car was tilted back with a heavy load in the trunk. He got out and opened the trunk, and it was full of fish. All kinds—sheepshead, jewfish, snook, trout, all kinds of fish. I'd never seen anything like it. He was a helluva fisherman.

"Man, where'd you get all these fish?" I asked.

"Marco Island," he said.

"Well, where in the hell is that?"

This I had to see. Next weekend we set out across the Trail (U.S. 41), me, Faye and Russell. We crossed the old swing bridge in Goodland, which was the only way across to Marco and Goodland in 1958. I fell in love when I crossed that bridge. I had such a funny feeling in my heart that I'd been here before. It was just unbelievable the feeling I had. We made our way onto the beach at Caxambas Pass over on Marco down by the tracking station. I bought bait from Herb Robinson, the guy who owned what is now Stan's Idle Hour not knowing that I'd ever buy that place or even have an offer to.

Back then, there was no development on Marco, nothing. There were three guys fishing there on the beach who were just leaving.

"You caught any snook?" I asked them. Our neighbor from Georgia told us snook was a prime fish we were likely to get on Marco,

"Just this little 14-inch one," one of them said. "You can have it if you want. It's not enough for us to keep."

"Yeah, I've got a wife and kids to feed. I'll take it," I said.

Faye and I cast our lines out. She had one of the cheap dime store models. No sooner had the other fishermen left, we started pulling 'em in. Our lines got crossed. We were both excited, jumping up and down. There were fishermen out in a boat laughing so hard I thought they would fall in the water. We must have been a sight.

Later, crossing over the bridge heading home, I looked around and said a prayer that I would say every time I crossed that bridge going back home to Miami:

"Lord, please let me come back here again." I was hooked.

≈ 2 ≈

GYPSIES ON THE MOVE

That Monday morning I reported to my supervisor and asked, "How about working me overtime on the weekend and then letting me have the next weekend off?" He agreed, and for about eleven years, 1958 to 1969, I was coming to Marco Island fishing every other weekend. I knew every Indian camp on the Trail. I had a buddy who felt the same way about Marco. God Almighty, we had a great time, fishing and sleeping on the beach. And many times Faye and the kids would come with us. That was just a great time in my life. It was so free, and it was just wonderful. I would always say that prayer when crossing the bridge.

Eventually we acquired a 16-foot boat and docked at the Idle Hour restaurant in Goodland. I had met—and bought bait from—the owner, Herb Robinson, and his wife, Betsy.

Along about 1968, I noticed a bulldozer on the island knocking down trees at the crossroads where the fire station is now at Bald Eagle and San Marco. After fishing for a while, I went back to the Idle Hour and asked Herb what was going on. With a sad look he said, "They're developing Marco Island."

Herb was an old Georgia cracker who had been here forever. He had been the bridge tender in the 1930s. His livelihood was taking big-shot bankers and business executives fishing. They would come because it was like the last frontier—isolated and remote. They would tip him well. Maybe they felt sorry for him. It was just real laid back. He would put them up in the motel across from the restaurant and they would bring their own linen. Herb saw his way of life passing away with the development of Marco Island coming.

So Herb said to me, "Stan, you like it here so much, why don't you buy this place?" Man, he had millionaires who wanted to buy his place, but he wouldn't sell it to them. He was offering it to me.

I thought about it for a second and said, "Herb, I've got three kids. I'm in debt for a car and a house. I work for the phone company making $175 a week. I'm just barely making it. I work overtime just to come fishing."

The months went by, and Herb kept on: "Will you buy this place?" One day he said, "Will you just buy the motel? I've got a first mortgage on it you can assume, and I'll give you a second mortgage at 5 percent interest. If you can come up with $10,000 you can have the motel."

It was a ten unit motel and I began to think about it. Herb told me he got $10 for double occupancy and $12 for a kitchen. I figured if there's 10 rooms, we'd have to live in two of them, so I'd have eight to rent. I thought if we were full half the month with those eight and the mortgage is a bit over $300, hell, we could make it. Also, I had bought my house in Miami in 1955. It was now 1968, so I had some equity built up.

After I had 20 years with that Southern Bell Telephone Company, they gave me two days off without pay once for "taking an extended break" one day. Now, bear in mind, I was trying to make a living, I got three small children, and we're not really making it that good, but we're hanging in.

Well, they said I took an hour break and they were watching me like the Gestapo or something. In 20 years, I'd always worked hard. It just floored me and hurt my feelings. But it certainly made me more willing to quit that job.

Soon I had 23 years with the phone company. I could retire after 30 years with it. But I said to Faye, "I want to quit the phone company, sell the house and buy that motel over there in Goodland and just do something for myself."

She said, "Are you crazy?"

I had a friend back then, a bachelor named Riley Summer who loved to spend time with my family. He said to Faye, "Faye you've got to let Stan do this. He's just himself when he's over there fishing. He's the hardest working guy I've ever seen. You got to trust him. He'll make a go of it."

He was right about me being so hard working. I put in more phones in Miami than anybody. We were evaluated every month, and I was generally number one, never less than third. The head boss was always taking me around to department heads and featuring me at banquets like I was somebody. I told them I didn't do it for that. I did it because I was just a hard worker.

Well Riley finally convinced Faye to let me sell the house to some Cubans and quit the phone company. On the trip over on July 9, 1969 we must have looked like a bunch of Gypsies running away from something. We came across that trail with two boats hooked up to two loaded-down cars with all our possessions moving into Goodland. It was a mess.

It took me and my boys three days with sling blades to cut away all the grass around the motel. You could hardly see the doors, it was so run down. It had artesian well water, the plumbing didn't work, the TVs didn't work. My wife cried for three months. She and I slept in Room 1, a kitchenette unit with a couch that made into a bed. The door opened to unit 2, and that's where the kids slept. It was the middle of summer, and there was no one to rent a room to.

We didn't rent a room from July to December. I exhausted 13 shares of AT&T stock and all our savings. And then I couldn't pay the light bill.

One day Riley came by to see us. He said, "Stan, how you doing?" I unburdened myself on him, told about the dire straits we were in.

"Well, how much do you need?" he asked.

"$200."

I knew in my heart that he didn't have any money to spare. But I let him write me a check for $200. I found out later that he got home and borrowed money from the credit union to cover the check. That's how good a friend he was.

I said, "I'll get even with you Riley."

"No, no," he said. "Just have a room for me any time I come over."

I said, "Aw, hell, you got that anyway. We're that good a friends."

So we get on our feet again, and one morning I got up and started shaving. I'd grown a beard, which, of course, the phone company would not allow. Faye said, "What are you doing?"

"I'm going up to Naples and get a job," I said. "I can't make it here, and I'm not going back to the phone company in Miami. I'm not going back."

In Naples I went to the United Telephone Company and met a guy who had quit the Bell system in Chicago. He and I hit it off real good. I tell him I need a job desperately and of course he sees all my experience.

He says, "OK, I'll see what I can do."

I said, "Sir, I don't want to be choosey, but can you let me work on Marco Island?"

Two weeks went by and he called me. "Stan I'm going to put you in charge of Marco Island, Isles of Capri and Everglades City. You'll have the new office in Marco and a truck."

So I went to work and we're catching up financially. Toward the end of December we finally rented a room in the motel. But Faye came to me one last time and said, "You know you really messed us up. You sold my house. You quit your job. You got me over here with these redneck fishermen and these construction workers. I'm not happy. I don't like it."

So I said to the good Lord, under my breath, "What can I do?" And He said to me "Say this," which I did.

I said, "Well honey, you know what? I made the biggest mistake of my life. Yes, I've sold our house, quit my job. I can't go back to the phone company, and I can't get the house back. I don't know what to do. What can we do?"

She said, "Well, I guess we'll just have to do the best we can."

It tears me up a little bit right now because then she kissed me. What a woman.

But it wasn't the first time I had dealt with hard times. I had come up that way.

≈ 3 ≈

COMING UP HARD

I was born April 30, 1926 at home in the country, about five or six miles outside of Bessemer, Alabama. Bessemer was a steel town—iron ore, steel, everything. I was born in an unpainted wooden house with the help of a midwife.

I remember being in that house maybe four or five years. It had lap siding, and, in the winter, our mother, Bertie Gober, would put newspapers in the cracks in the walls.

I had two brothers—Wally, 13 months older than me, and Floyd, four years younger than me—and a sister, Vera, who was the oldest.

We moved to another place close by. My grandmother and grandfather on my mother's side, Bertie Missouri Harris and J.B. Harris lived in that same neighborhood. The little community there was called "Dogtown." I don't know why. I just heard them say that when I was little.

In 1930, when I was four years old, my dad left. He left my mother with us four kids to raise. My mother had to be on welfare to get along through the Great Depression. The one thing that helped us a lot was that one of my mother's sisters, who worked for the phone company as an operator, moved in with us for a long time, till I became a teenager.

For the next 12 years, we were on welfare. My mother's father had a good job in a foundry and they helped us as best they could.

So we moved around and finally ended up in another little wooden unpainted house in Bessemer. I guess we were kind of outcasts because it was the only house in the whole neighborhood that was like that. All the rest of them were painted, with nice trimmed hedges, sidewalks and stuff. We had all that, but the house didn't look good.

We lived around there for a long while and then moved again. I think we moved a total of about six times around Bessemer because my mother was on her own now and trying her best to keep us going. I think we moved so much because we couldn't pay the rent—every time it came due we had to move. And there's four of us kids. On top of taking care of us, my mother took in washings and ironings and also took care of a sick old fellow. She'd go and sit with him at times. In her way she worked hard and kept us going.

Every time we moved to a new school, it seemed like all the guys wanted to jump me and beat me up because I was a scrubby looking little guy who wore "welfare clothes." So I had my share of getting beat up, I'll tell you that. Kids are kids, and they pick on other adverse kids, I suppose. Maybe it made me a better person.

So here we are on welfare, my mother's got four kids and no husband. Somebody had to grow up quick.

My sister, Vera, was the oldest, but my grandparents on my mother's side took care of her because she was a girl and she got everything they could give her. Well, my brother, Wally, who's 13 months older than me, had to grow up at the age of 15. He just had to. He got a job in a restaurant called Acme Lunch, and joined a Young Man's Christian Association, and he dressed nice and was walking a straight line.

Acme Lunch was a lunch counter with 26 stools. People would actually stand behind each other, waiting on people to get through eating to get a seat. Acme Lunch served country food with a steam table—meatloaf, chicken, hamburgers, barbecue, all that good stuff. They needed a cook, so Wally told them our mother was a good one, and they hired her.

I was about 12 then and my younger brother, Floyd, we called him Butch, and I used to sell the Sunday paper on the street in downtown Bessemer for about a penny a paper. But then Acme Lunch gave me a job washing dishes.

Two gentlemen, Virgil Blake and Jimmy Vines, owned Acme Lunch. I didn't have a father anymore to guide me and my mother was working all the time to try to keep her family going, so she didn't keep up with us a lot. The thing that helped me the most in my young life that I didn't even know was helping me was that these two men I worked for were honest men. I *never* heard them down anyone or refuse to help anyone that needed something. They sponsored a basketball team in my hometown and a baseball team.

I went out for football in about 8th grade. Back then, I weighed only 111 pounds. There was the first team, second team, third team and the scrub team. I was on the scrub team for a year, then the next year I weighed 131 pounds and I got up to the next team. We got to play other high schools around Jefferson County, Alabama, which is where Birmingham is, and we traveled a little bit and played in other schools. The greatest thrill of my little football career as a left half-back was when I actually scored one touchdown. What a thrill!

After a couple of years at Acme Lunch, in 1941 when the U.S. is headed for the war, I graduated to the counter, and my brother graduated to working the short-order grill. Eventually, they taught me how to work the grill too.

So, with my mother and brother cooking at Acme and me washing dishes, we got off welfare.

I just want to say we had the greatest mother in the world. God bless her. I know she is in heaven. Thank you mother for love and for keeping us together.

≈ 4 ≈

MY SHINING HOUR

Before you know it, I'm 17 years old and in the 10th grade. While I had good steady work at Acme Lunch, I spent my extra time singing at my high school, going to recitals and what not. I had a buddy named Kenneth Carr. We learned a lot of different songs because he could read music. We got all the latest songs from the ten cent store. Back in those days the big stars were Bing Crosby, Perry Como, Nat King Cole.

Well, a guy from the Gary Hotel (just around the corner in downtown Bessemer) named Ron Faulkner ate lunch at Acme every day, and he was the announcer on radio station WJLD, Bessemer, Alabama.

One day Ron said, "You wanna sing on the radio? I know you're singin' all around high school, and goin' around to those recitals."

He offered to give me 15 minutes on-air Wednesday night. So I agreed. Suddenly, I'm like a little celebrity of the town because I'm on the radio, and all them little girls, man!

Back in those days, everybody hung out at Walgreens on the corner. They had a big soda fountain and booths, and all the kids sat in there and drank sodas. There wasn't all that dope and drinking back in those days. We grew up slow. And I don't think that was too bad.

So at Walgreens, they would all tune in to the radio when I was singing, and I'd go by there and they'd fix me up some lime drink for my throat, and, oh, they just petted me around. It was a great time.

I sang on the radio two or three months. Our theme song was "This Will Be My Shining Hour," a Sinatra song. This was in 1944, and Sinatra was coming on strong. Perry Como, The Bing, those were the people I liked. We'd start out by singin':

> "This will be my shining hour / Calm and happy and
> bright like the light shinin' before me / There's an angel
> standin' before me / This will be my shining hour / 'til we
> meet again."

We'd take time for that at the start and end of the show. We just did popular songs with the piano player. In the 15 minutes we'd get in four to six songs.

World War II was going on at this point. At Acme Lunch, we had to slice the buns to get ready for lunch. We'd line up new, clean garbage cans and slice garbage cans full of buns. On December 7, 1941, Jimmy Vines (one of Acme's owners) and I were slicing buns when the Japs attacked Pearl Harbor. Jimmy knew I would have to go to war because I would soon be eligible.

He said, "Stan, I wouldn't worry about them Japs if I was you." (He's got that big knife swinging.) "I'd just go out there and kill me about a dozen 'fore lunch and take the rest of the day off."

That stuck with me ever since. And, of all the things, they sent me to the Pacific.

≈ 5 ≈

"SQUARE THAT HAT, SAILOR"

I went up to City Hall to join the Navy 15 days before I was 18 years old. When I got there, the guy said to me, "What's your name, son?"

I said, "Stanley Gober."

He said, "What's your middle name?"

I said, "I don't have a middle name."

He said, "Listen, I need your middle name."

Now, I really didn't have one. So I said, "But I don't have a middle name." He said, "Listen, boy. We gotta war goin' on heah and we got no time for no bullshit. Now gimme a damn middle name, and by God I mean NOW!"

Jimmy Vines' wife, Virginia Vines, also worked at Acme Lunch, and she never called me Stan. She always called me "S.R." I don't know to this day *why*. She'd say, "S.R., come here," "S.R., clean this . . ." "S.R., get this . . ."

Well, standing there at City Hall, all of a sudden I thought of "S.R.," and for some reason I thought of *Russell*. So I said, "Russell."

He said, "That with two Ls ?"

"Yes Sir."

So, I enlisted in the Navy as Stanley Russell Gober and got in April 15, 1944.

My brother, Wally, joined the Navy half a year before I did. He too was in the Pacific. The only difference between us was that he was in action, and I never was. He served around the islands close to Japan on an ammunition ship, and, brother, was he scared! The Japanese dropped bombs all around one of the bays he was in. In fact, his boat even caught fire, and they scrambled to put it out.

Two months after joining the Navy and training in Williamsburg, Virginia, I went overseas. We took a troop train all the way from Virginia to San Francisco and shipped out of there.

I ended up on a hospital base in Noumea. It was Fleet Hospital #105, Noumea, New Caledonia. I was the lucky one. I was there 16 months, and the only Jap I saw was a prisoner of war we kept at the hospital. The Navy hired a local native, a Kanaky, which was the term favored by the Melanesians, to guard the prisoner. They let the Japanese prisoner fish for octopus on the beach with a little throw net. The big black Kanaky was built like Superman, had a big bolo knife and he would walk up and down the beach waving that knife. There was no way the Jap prisoner, who probably weighed 140 pounds was going to try to get away from him.

I stayed there the duration of the war.

Overseas we didn't have to worry about the rules too much. One rule was to always wear our Navy cap the width of two fingers above the eyebrows. The war was over by 1945, and I was 19 years old and headed home on a 10-day leave.

Standing in the pay line in Charleston, South Carolina, my hat was back a little bit on my head. An officer saw me and told me to square my hat, which I did, no problem.

As the line moved up, we're chit-chatting. I'm excited about going home for the first time since being overseas, and I absent-mindedly slide my hat back a little. That same officer sees me again and goes berserk, shouting, "*I told you to square that hat, sailor!*"

He brought another officer over and told him to put me on clean-the-barracks detail for the weekend. I said, "But sir, I've got a 10-day leave to go home."

"Cancel his leave," he said. "Put him on barracks detail for the weekend."

I had to spend the weekend scrubbing the barracks with a mop and bucket. So I went to the chief and said, "Chief, please get my leave back for me." I had done some favors for the chief, and he fixed it so I could go on leave.

Always trying to entertain, I was in two shows in the Navy. In New Caledonia, I was in the chorus line, of all things. A lot of entertainers came over to the Pacific—Bob Hope, Jack Benny, Martha Tilton, Francis Langford, Jerry Calona. I mean all great singers and entertainers. Jackie Cooper played drums. Two sets of drums—he sat in the middle and played them both.

They'd have these shows, but we'd also put on shows locally, for the troops on the base. I was the lead "chorus girl" of about four Navy guys. Singin' "These pu-r-r-t-y gir-r-rls are like a melodyyyy . . ." That was one, another one was, "Dancin' in the rain." They made us up with wigs and short little skirts and garters. At the end when we danced out, we'd take the garter off and throw it to the audience. Man, I'll never forget that.

≈ 6 ≈

GIRL WATCHING

I went into the Navy April 15, 1944, and I came out May 15, 1946. I came back to San Francisco, then got discharged in New Orleans. I surprised my mother and just came walking up the back steps one day, and, oh, they like to fainted! They knew I was getting out, but they didn't know when. Needless to say, everybody cried.

Mother was still working at Acme Lunch. Virgil Blake had sold Acme Lunch to Jimmy Vines, because Virgil was a supervisor in the National Bridge Company, a steel company in Bessemer. Jimmy had then gotten sick with lung cancer. He never smoked, but he put so much time in over the grill that they attributed that to his cancer.

When Jimmy died, his wife, Virginia, took over at Acme. She ran it the best way she could, but she never really liked doing it. So she asked my mother if she wanted to buy the restaurant.

Now here we are, mother's got no money—none of us have. But the people in this little town thought so much of her and how she treated them and how honest she was that the banker just loaned her the whole $7,000 that she needed, and she bought the place. In 1946 that was quite a lot of money.

Wally had learned to be a baker while in the Navy. So he got a job at a local bakery decorating cakes. He lasted about two years, but he couldn't get California out of his mind. He had gotten married and had a child. So he just packed up everything, got on a train and went to San Diego. (He ended up retiring from Sears/Allstate in San Diego after 30 years.)

I got a job with the phone company in 1947. All the phone guys used to eat at Acme—the foreman and the supervisor included. They always said, "Them boys get out of the service, we'll give 'em a job."

I worked at the phone company every day and cooked every night at Acme. I'd get off from the phone company at 5 p.m., take a shower and head to the restaurant, where I'd relieve my mother, sending her home. I'd cook from 6 p.m. till close at 10 p.m. I did that for five years. I even cooked over my vacation time. I built up two weeks, and I'd take that at Christmas because of the heavy traffic that came to town.

In those days, everybody came to town on Saturday night. It was just a way of life. It was almost like going back into the western days. Everybody would come to town on Saturday night, and on Sunday they'd go to the lake or something like that.

Girl watching was a big thing in those days. Guys would sit in their cars and watch the girls go by. Everybody washed their car every week, and you were so proud of your car. If you were a Chevy man, then you hated Ford people. And the Ford people hated you. And you all tried to outdo each other with the flaps and the fender covers and the different lights on the back. I remember when I had a guy put a little round stop light on the back of my '49 Chevy. It was one of those humpback deals that went straight down—oh, it was beautiful!

≈ 7 ≈

I MET HER AT A FIVE AND
TEN CENT STORE

The war was over, and I had a good job at the phone company. Then I met a gal, Mary Lee Welch, at the ten cent store. I would often think of that song that Bing Crosby made famous: "I Met Her in a Five and Ten Cent Store." She came from a family out in the country. Her father was a farmer. I dated her almost a year and I could never go into their house. I could only take her to the door. I never even met her father! He was that grumpy of a man.

We got married in 1947, and we had a little girl the third year of our marriage. Rebecca Lee was born September 18, 1950.

I worked for the phone company, for mother at the restaurant, and I ran a softball stadium concession stand two nights of the week. I had my own little softball team, and I had a lot of energy. I was enjoyin' things.

I built a little one-bedroom house on a long lot—175 by 100 feet. I built it on the back with the understanding that one day I'd build a house on the front and rent that. So I divided it off with a fence and had plenty of property.

Well, our marriage fell apart. It wasn't any fault of hers or mine—

except that she was actually in love with her high school sweetheart. She had come up in a broken home where the mother and father didn't get along. So now I come along in her life, and she latches onto me, I think because she wants to get out of the environment she's in.

But she finally realized she's still in love with her high school sweetheart. So she finally took a job in a big super food store, and her sweetheart was working in the meat department of that store. Now, I'm not saying there was hanky-panky because she was a good person.

She just told me one day that we were having a little problem in the bed, and I said, "I just don't understand you, what's wrong?"

And she finally told me, "Y'know what Stan? I don't really love you."

I said, "You *what?* After all this? We have a little girl!"

She said, "I really don't."

We were so bad with our sex life and being young people, I had her go to the doctor, and I went too. He examined both of us. He said to me, "There's nothin' wrong with you, there's nothin' wrong with her. Whatever it is, is in her mind."

So that's what it was. She was in love with somebody else.

We got the same attorney. I told Mary Lee, "Well, you know, if it's over, it's over. I'm not gonna have a damn fit," which I didn't. I knew I couldn't keep our daughter because Mary Lee was such a good mother and housekeeper. She was really neat and clean, sewed clothes. She just absolutely had been taught and was good.

There was no way I would even try to take Becky away from her. So we agreed I could see her any time, for any reasonable length of time and she could stay with me if she elected to in the summers when school was out.

We had $700 in the bank, believe it or not. I gave it to Mary Lee so she could buy a car. I gave her the house. I took my car, moved back to my mother's and started all over.

≈ 8 ≈

THE LOVE OF MY LIFE
WALKS IN

So after Mary Lee and I split up, I just focused on working hard at the phone company and at the restaurant for my mother. And one Sunday afternoon Faye R. Campbell came in there. I think it's an old story, but when I saw her, it was just *something*, you know?

Well, I just came around the counter from the grill and sat right down by her. I said, "How you doin'?" She said, "OK." She was only 16 or maybe 17. She was young.

I said, "Well, you sure are pretty." She said, "Whadda ya? Whadda ya?" you know. She really didn't want anything to do with me.

It was in the summer, and she had on shorts. I was carried away with her. I said things to her that I just don't know what made me say them, like, "My God, you've got pretty legs." And she looked at me like, "I ain't gonna have nothin to do with this crazy guy!" I was nine years older than her.

I said, "Y'know I'm gonna get off here in a little bit. Would you like to take a walk down in the park?"

She said, "God no! I don't even know you!"

I said, "Well, I know, but we could get to know each other." I was putting her on, but it wasn't working. I was just crazy, man!

As time went by, I couldn't get her out of my mind. Down the street from us, there was a restaurant called Lared's. It was an actual restaurant—not a coffee counter like Acme. I went out to Lared's one day, and Faye was working in there as a waitress.

I said, "Well, I'll be damned, look at this, will ya?" And she *still* wouldn't have anything to do with me.

Ron Robuck, one of the guys who worked with me at the phone company, was kind of a go-getter and he started dating one of the girls that worked in Lared's.

Two nights a week I also ran a softball concession stand—just Cokes, potato chips, cookies and the like. I had guys who helped me with the stand. Ron was dating this gal who worked at Lared's, and one night he pulled up down at the softball field and ran up there to the concession. He said, "C'mon Stan! I got Faye in the car!"

I said, "Really?!"

Now my catcher's name was Armstrong—good catcher. So I say, "Armstrong, take over. Man, I'm gone!"

The only way I got be with Faye was when Ron brought her. Ron tricked her. He had his girlfriend in the car and he said he was going to take her home and he'd drop Faye off too. Instead, he came to the softball stadium.

I ran over there so fast and got in the back seat with her, and I never will forget, she said, "Man, you got hands like an octopus." I'm all over her, you know.

So we started dating. In our hometown, back in those days, the street car ran through town. It ran out in the rurals and different places. But right in the middle of town was the street car. One time—I don't know why or what made me do it—but she was on the street car going home, and I had a little pickup truck. I flagged that street car down and got her off the damn street car and drove her home myself.

≈ 9 ≈

FAYE AND I HEAD SOUTH

Faye R. Campbell and I ended up getting married in Mississippi. (She never let me tell anyone her middle name, which was Ruby.) Not long after that, on December 3, 1952, Sammy Russell came along.

After divorcing Mary Lee, I moved back in with my mother, who loved me dearly. I had a step-father now. It wasn't a good move. He wasn't a bad guy, but I was just infringing on their life. Then I married Faye, and we've got this little baby boy, and that makes it worse, even though mother loved her little grandson.

Time goes by, and we're not really happy because I'm not doing well. I'm working, but at the same time we all left mother in the restaurant. She started losing money and she just couldn't pay the bills. I think some of the people who worked for her were stealing her blind out the back door. She just couldn't be there all the time, and she was getting older too.

I'm still with the phone company, so I had good credit. I bailed her out somewhat. I got a loan for her, but her situation just didn't get better. She had to go to debtor's court, and she paid off all her bills. Then she started working at one of the schools running the cafeteria, which worked out well for her. She retired from that.

We were still in kind of a bad situation at home. My mother loved me dearly, so she wouldn't say, "Stan, you need to leave," but I'm figuring this isn't working. One day in 1954, they put a bid on the bulletin board at work—"Anyone wanting to transfer to Miami, Fort Lauderdale, or West Palm Beach, Florida, submit a bid because they're booming down there and the south is not."

So, I told Faye, let's go to Miami, the biggest city down there, and try our luck." I had seven years with the phone company, so I got the bid.

Russ was very little then, maybe 16 months. On the drive down to Miami, we took Highway 27, and I had never seen so many lakes in my life. I'll never forget little Russ standing up in the seat saying, "Wa-wa. Wa-Wa." He wanted to get in one of those lakes. That was just funny as hell. I guess he was destined to be a fisherman or something.

In Miami, we rented a few different places, and we had a stroke of bad luck right quick. Faye got very sick with female trouble, and the doctors in Miami wouldn't accept the Blue Cross Blue Shield that we had with the Bell System because it hadn't transferred from Alabama to Florida yet.

They looked me in the eye and said she needed a D&C, a female operation, and we needed to pay $500 up front. I told them I didn't have the money, but that I do have insurance that just hadn't transferred. They told me that if the insurance came through they'd reimburse me. I told them that wouldn't work. So her uncle (her mother's brother) came down and packed her up in the car, and took her back to Bessemer. Since the insurance was still in Alabama, they operated on her there.

They took Russ too, so I was down in Miami by myself having a hard time when, of all things, my car breaks down—*major*. Timing chain. I left it on a vacant lot by my place. I couldn't move it, I had no money, I had to ride a bus to work, and I was eating at the Royal Castle—a hamburger for lunch, chili for supper.

Nobody knew me, nobody was friendly. It was one of the worst times of my life. I was so lonesome.

Faye finally got better, and I went to Alabama to see her. I drove all the way up there in an old Hudson. Oh man, it was unbelievable too. It rattled, but I made it.

While I was up there, I got to see my real dad for the first time as a grown adult. He had married another gal and moved to Boston. I have three half-sisters and a half-brother from Boston. We all know and love each other. Two of them live in Naples now.

So my dad and I meet at a bar in Bessemer and have a drink together. Faye's with me, but she's real skinny because she's been through a lot. He picked her little skinny arm up and had the audacity to say, "Boy, you gotta get some meat on this woman!" I'm thinking, "She's been in the hospital, are you crazy?"

After Faye got out of the hospital, we got back down to Miami. Now I was really homesick for Alabama. I was trying to go back there. The phone company told me they'd let me transfer back if I was real serious.

In the meantime, the last G.I. Housing project came available in Miami. It was a beautiful project by a school—a three bedroom house. So I borrowed $100 from a guy, and put it down for that house.

Now when we got this house, I knew I had to give up going back to Alabama because Faye was thrilled to death with this house, and she didn't want to go back to Alabama. I'm locked in. We have a mortgage, and we have this house.

Russ is about 6 years old, and Jay Carlton came along November 2, 1957. Steve Patrick would be born on October 12, 1965.

Now, about my kids' names: When Sammy Russell (Russ) was born, Faye said, "You can't name him Sammy. It's got to be Sam or Samuel."

I said, "No, by God, I'm namin' him Sammy Russell."

She asked, "Why?"

"My middle name, of course, and Sammy for the professional football player, Sammy Barr from Texas." I said.

Jay Carlton was born and Faye wanted to know why his name was Jay. I thought everybody knew about Jay Berwanger the first winner of the Heisman Trophy.

When Steve Patrick was born, naturally she asked me who Steve was. Of course he was named after Steve Sloan the Alabama quarterback, victorious in the Orange Bowl on January 1, 1966.

I named all three of my boys after football players. I always liked football even though I wasn't big enough to play.

In our Miami days, I was still into entertaining. I sang anywhere I found a piano bar. Also at work I was elected chairman of the entertainment committee for the Communication Workers of America union. We put on some good shows.

Then I met a guy who was an emcee for a lot of shows around Miami, and he'd get me on some of those shows.

I was on some good shows. I was on the Rose Ball at the City Pier Auditorium—with class acts. I was scared to death! I sang, "You'll never know just how much I love you . . ." with a full orchestra. And there were roses from South America, all different colors. Man, it was a great show, a great program!

There was an opera singer in there from Paris. And another great thing, Sandy Worth, she was the Orange Bowl Queen of that year, 1958 or '59. She did the baton that was on fire on each end, and she put on a show with that. Great stuff.

I got a show down in Dinner Key Auditorium on St. Patrick's Day. Lord, what a mess that was. I sang Elvis' "Love Me Tender," and there were four drunk Irishmen trying to get on the stage to sing with me. The cops were trying to get them out of there. That was a rough time.

I tried to get on TV down there, but the guys would never let me. They'd say, "You gotta have experience." I'd tell 'em I'd been singin' all around, here and there, but they said I needed more and then to come back. So I said, "How am I gonna get experience if you don't give me a chance?" But they never would.

So we're rocking along in Miami, and things are better. I got another car, we're catching up with our bills. I'm working a lot of overtime.

Then, in 1958, the fisherman from Georgia who led me to Marco Island moved into my neighborhood, and our lives were never the same.

≈ 10 ≈

GET OUTTA MY YARD

Before moving from Miami, I prayed to God to show me something else to do because I wanted to get away from the phone company. Moving to Goodland and taking that chance with three kids and buying that motel was all based on a prayer. My prayer every night was, "Please show me something else to do." And He did.

After some hardship with the motel in Goodland, I got that phone company job in Naples. They let me work on Marco Island, gave me a truck and everything. I started making money with that phone company, and we could pay the notes on the motel.

Christmas time, 1969, came around. We were renting some more rooms, and I went over to the Olde Marco Inn and sang some songs with a piano player named Meredith Green.

In January, 1970, here came Herb Robinson again from across the street. He said, "Stan, why don't you buy my restaurant and the five lots on the water?"

Now, Faye still wasn't exactly pleased with our new life at this point.

I said, "Herb, I'm going to tell you something. My wife hates me. The kids are looking at me funny. You're going to have to get out of the yard, man, cause I can't handle it. I'm in debt $60,000. I'm so screwed up you can't believe it. I'm not fixin' to buy nothing else. I think you better just get on outta my yard!"

He did. But then Faye overheard us and came over to me. "Stan what did you do that for?"

I said, "Well, hell, honey, you're not happy. We're in debt. And what would we do with a restaurant? That's really hard work. I know. I grew up in one in Alabama. I told mom I'd *never* do that again. And where would we get the money anyway?"

But Faye took it upon herself to ask anybody who came into Goodland looking like they might have some money if they would loan us $10,000 so we could take on two more mortgages.

So here we go again.

Well, a guy comes down from Ross Common, Michigan, named Lexie Herron. He was a millionaire who was a workin' man all his life, a business person. He was also a master carpenter at age 69. At the time I was 42. He was renting a room at the motel, and we became good friends.

In the meantime, I had an appointment with Naples Federal and Loan where Herb Robinson had the first mortgage on the motel and the restaurant. I went in and talked to the vice president. I told him my deal. I had bought the motel and spent eight months making all the payments and fixing the place up, and now I wanted to take on the restaurant too. I didn't have any additional collateral to give him.

He said there was just no way the directors would go along with it without additional money.

I said, "Sir, I'm the workingest SOB you've ever seen. And I guarantee I'll die before I beat you. In fact I'll give you a life insurance policy on my life to back up the loan."

He said, "I believe you, but the board just won't go along."

He said he knew a rich fellow in Naples who sometimes financed a deal like this, and he said he'd talk to him and get back to me.

So I went on back to Goodland somewhat dejected. Lexie had gotten wind of the possible deal on the restaurant. He saw me and said, "Boy, (he always called me "boy") did you get your money?"

"No sir, I got no collateral," I said. "They won't loan me the money."

Lexie said, "Boy, I'm going to loan you $10,000. I believe you can make it."

Before we could get all the paperwork together, Lexie went back to Ross Common. He left me his unlisted phone number so I could call him to wire the money. Well, I lost the phone number. We were ready to close the deal, but I had no way to get in touch with Lexie.

I scratched my head and said a prayer. "Lord, what am I going to do?" And He said to me "You know Ross Common must not be too big a town since you've never heard of it before. And since Lexie was a master carpenter, surely someone at the hardware store or lumber company would know his number."

With that bit of inspiration from the Lord, I got the phone number of the lumber company in Ross Common. As I was dialing the number, I got to thinking. This town is way up in yankee country. I'm from Alabama. I had better talk really fast so they'll think I'm one of them.

A guy answered the phone:

"RossCommonHardware&LumberCompany."

"HeyGimmeTheNumberForLexyHerronWillya?"

"OK."

I called Lexie. He sent the money and we did the deal. I never charged Lexie for anything after that. He called me "boy" until the day he died in 1984 at age 83.

Lex wanted his money paid back in five years, but he wanted the interest between the time of the loan and five years, which we agreed to. Of course, we figured it this way: The Mackle brothers were developing Marco at the time, and every time they put an ad in the paper, we clapped our hands—we're going under if they go under. So we saved and struggled. Well, in one year and eight months we paid him back out of a brown paper sack. Baby, that was a great day! We both got drunk, I can tell you that!

So in 1970, I had five mortgages and was back in the restaurant business.

≈ 11 ≈

PUTTING IN A BAR

So we're swinging along with this little restaurant in about 1974, and we've got the boat charters coming in, and we have the motel. We have a lot of debt, but we're paying it. The good Lord's blessing us.

Well, there's this big vacant room on the right side of the restaurant facing it, a big playroom with a pool table that went with the restaurant. Through a little open window in it, you could serve food through there. Mostly it was for the kids and the young people to play pool after they got out of school, because there was nothing to do around Goodland.

A guy called me one day and said there's a bar right behind the phone company, the Coconut Bar, that had some extra bar stuff to get rid of. (The Coconut Bar was so quaint that they put their customers' names on their stools.) I went over to check it out, and they had five or six barstools, an upright freezer that they kept the beer mugs in, a beer cooler, and the bar itself—a little 90-degree counter that these barstools set around. The guy would take $500 for all of it. I wasn't really thinking seriously of going into the bar business. Still, we had the restaurant, but all we had was beer and wine.

So we bought the bar stuff from the Coconut Bar and put it all in the vacant room with the pool table. Faye said, "Why don't you set it up and we'll have a little bar in here?" I never thought of *that*. I said, "Yeah, that ain't a bad idea!"

So we set that little bar up. We had a back entrance to come into the room, so it was perfect. I put the beer cooler in and put the freezer against the wall. We got some cold beer, put it in the cooler, and plugged it in.

All of a sudden one guy come in, "So what's goin' on here?"

"Oh, we gotta little bar here," I said. So one of us stayed in there in between cooking in the restaurant. We took in $16 the first night. I'll never forget that as long as I live!

We eventually added on to it, put shelves around, made the bar bigger, and took that pool table and traded it for a juke box and a pay-per-round pool table. So now, we're in the bar business. So on the wall we just write, "chicken basket," "shrimp basket," "oyster basket"—we're in business, man!

Finally we got the restaurant going good. We were living upstairs then. The money people started moving to Marco thanks to the Mackle brothers. So there're really goin' at it. That's one reason that made me want to quit the phone company and go in debt with the restaurant.

Now, Faye said to me, "You know what, Stan? With all these people moving in on Marco and the money coming in, and the restaurants springing up, I don't think we're gonna be able to make it unless we get a liquor license. We need it bad. We've got this seafood restaurant on the water, we got beer and wine, but we got no liquor."

Nobody had a liquor license except the ones with the quota license, like the Marco Barge. A quota license is the one where you can have a package and you can sell stuff to go. We only had a restaurant license, so we really had to watch for people taking a drink out, or even bringing one in.

So I said, "Faye, if you would run the restaurant, to keep all this off of my head as much as possible, then I'll go to war with the county to try to get this liquor license." I knew it'd be a battle. And it was. It seemed like every possible government official from the county all the way up to Tallahassee had to be appeased to get his approval.

It took me seven or eight months of fighting from Naples to Fort Myers. And my fight was, "We have the property, we have the building, whatever we have to do I'll do."

Well, the powers that be said, "You gotta put in enough seating for 200 people, you gotta have enough knives, forks, spoons, glasses, cups, for 200 people. Your building's gotta be 600 square feet, you gotta park 200 cars."

So I found an architect on Marco, and he drew all the parking for me. I borrowed $37,000.

Lexie built the upstairs dining room. We had to take out the pool tables and all that stuff to put in dining room furniture. So now we're out of the pool business. (A certain amount of trouble comes with pool tables anyway. We didn't have a lot of fights, but we did have some confrontations with people.)

We put in everything we needed for the liquor license, and the bureaucrats still fight with me over it. My theme was: "Listen. I'm an American. I was in the Second World War. I've got the property, I got the seating. *Why* won't you let me have the liquor license?"

They said, "Because you're on a septic tank."

I said, "*A septic tank?!* Hell, you want me to build a sewer?!"

They said, "No." See, the septic tank is on an oyster shell mound out there. Well, there was one old feller in the county who had been there when Herb and Betsy Robinson built the place in the '50s. He got wind of all this, and he went and told the county that the septic tank has never been pumped out. That helped me, but they still sent me to Fort Myers to get OK'd by a guy up there.

This guy was a purebred Englishman. He talked like he was right out of London. Well, I got a little bit hyper with him, and I stood up over him and I said, "Y'know what?! I don't understand dammit! I'm gonna go under if you guys don't award me the liquor license. I'm willing to pay for what I'm gettin'. I'm not asking for a handout. But there's so much money moving on Marco and people from up north, out west, wherever they're comin' from, they got a lot of money. I ain't got no money. I'm in debt. I need cocktails, so we'll have that to offer the people that come there, see."

I was hovering over him while he was sitting at his desk, and I said, "Now they sent me up here, and told me it was up to *you!*" He was nervous. I would never have hit the guy, but maybe he thought I would.

He got on the phone and called the health department in Naples and he said, "Mr. G-G-Gober's here. He-he-he said you guys said it's up to me." See, he'd been trying to tell me it was up to them, so I'm getting the runaround. So he said, "OK, alright, we'll do that."

He hung up the phone and says, "OK, Mr. Gober, we're going to get you the liquor license, but, with that septic tank you have there, and the increased traffic that you may get, we're going to demand that you only open for the dinner hour, not for lunch."

I'd already given up breakfast because it was just wearing me and Faye down. So I said, "OK, sure, that's great." Of course I walked out of there and I said to myself, "Ain't no damn way I'm gonna give up lunch! These idiots ain't gonna know what I'm doin' anyway!"

Two weeks go by. Nothing. I call the guy. "This is Stan. Where's my approval at?" "Oh-oh, I'm gonna mail them today!" he said. And he did.

So now we added onto the building, and a guy comes over from Lauderdale from the hotel/restaurant state association. He has to OK the silverware, all the dishes, all the chairs and all the tables. Then we got this guy that OK'd the building. How it's built. This guy comes over—he was a smart ass—he said, "You got 200 chairs, you got all this, all that?"

"Yes, sir, you can count 'em. Got 'em all."

He said, "Well, you know what, I can't OK this."

I said, "*Why not?!*"

He said, "Because those stairs out there gotta be fireproof."

I said, "Fireproof? Listen, I done spent all the money we got! What do you mean by fireproof?!"

He said, "Like metal or blocks." They were wooden.

I said, "Oh, my God!" And he left.

We got the bar upstairs and everything. We're ready. It looks good too. I'm sitting there bitching about it all. We got beer and wine but no liquor. So my son, Jay, said, "Dad, why don't you paint the steps with fireproof paint?" I said, "Jay, I don't need no bullshit, OK? I'm already upset anyway." Some guy sittin' there drinkin' beer says, "Y'know, that ain't no bad idea." I said, "Really?" So I called Sherwin Williams in Naples and they had fireproof paint that was supposed to give you 15 to 20 minutes to get out of the building.

I said, "Well, I'll be damned!"

The guy who OK'd the construction was there one day, and I said to him, "Y'know, this guy that does this other part, he's a damn asshole. He treats me like an idiot."

He said, "Ya, ya, he is an asshole. I'll tell you what. If he gives you any more trouble, here's my card. You call me."

I'd never met this guy in my life. He had to have been in his 70s. Later on, I called him and told him the problem with fireproofing the stairs.

He said, "That's his reason?"

I said, "Yessir. He even showed me in the book"

He said, "Well, let me ask ya something, Stan. What did that book look like?"

I said, "Well, it's about eight inches long and four inches in width and maybe three-quarters of an inch thick, or something like that." He said he'd call me back.

He called me back in less than 30 minutes. He said, "You go ahead Stan with your business. He'll be over there and okay it."

I said, "My God! Sir, what did you do?"

He said, "Well, when you told me what book that was and what it looked like . . . See, we have various books that we go by over here. We got new books, we got reconstruction books, remodelin' books. We got all kinds." He said, "That stairway was there, and it shows it on your print when you started this thing. That's an existing stairway and that is approved. That's existing. It had nothing to do with you."

Boy, that fireproof stairs jerk came back over. He says, "You got two hun'erd chairs?" I said, "Ya." "Two hun'erd settings?" I said, "Yes, sir. Ya." "You got this that and the other. . . ?" I said, "Ya, got ever'thang."

He said, "Okay. Can I use your phone?" And this is about what killed me. He called Tallahassee and said, "This is number so-in-so" and I thought, "You son-of-a-gun, you. That's all you are is a number." And he said in the phone, "Stan Gober's ready for his license." They said, "Okay."

I asked him when I'd get my license. He said Tallahassee would mail it to me when the director signs the papers, probably in a couple of weeks." Well, I waited and, hell, nobody and nothing. So I called the beverage department in Tallahassee and told them I've got some liquor licenses that might be ready. The lady I spoke to said they were on the director's desk and as soon as he signed them, they'd mail them to me.

I asked to speak to that director. I said, "Sir, I'm down in Southwest Florida and I'm really waitin' on my liquor license and I just wondered if you know when you're gonna sign the license, 'cause I could come up and get 'em."

He said, "I'll sign them when I get to it!" The jerk.

I said, "I just wanna know 'cause it's gonna take me eight hours to get there."

"Well, I'll sign 'em and we'll let you know when they're signed," he said.

Ain't this the shits? Son-of-a-bitch calls me back at 3:30 p.m. His secretary says, "The director signed your license. Do you want to pick 'em up or do you want us to mail them?"

Now, if they mail them to me, I've got to mail a check back to them, then they got to mail the license back to me. We're talking about another two or three weeks.

I said, "Ma'am, no. I'll come get 'em tomorrow." So I said, "Russ, take over. Me and Steve (he was just a little kid, 6 years old), we gonna go to Tallahassee."

So Faye, Steve and I got in the car, and we drove to Tallahassee. We were so excited to get a liquor license. Nobody had liquor but the Marco Beach Hotel and the Barge. We got to Tallahassee, and I walked up to the counter, said, "I come to get the liquor license." "Oh yes," the lady said, "I got 'em ready right here. It'll be so-much money." I gave them a cashier's check.

Now we got the license, and we're happy.

We headed back to Goodland down Highway 27, and we had enough money for what we thought would set the bar up. So we stopped at an ABC Liquor store somewhere on the highway and went in there. There were two guys just hanging around in there, and they didn't say a word to me. They kept talking to each other.

I said, "Hey! You know what? I got five hun'erd dollars to spend 'cause I'm settin' up a bar. Will one of you guys help me?"

"WHOA! God, yessir! What can we do for you?!"

I said, "Well, I'll tell you what. I'm new in the bar business, but I know I need bar booze and I need top-shelf booze. So will you guys help me?"

We got four grocery carts full of booze and filled the trunk of the car with it.

Faye and I are in the car coming on down the highway, and we're still excited. I said, "Boy wouldn't it be nice to have a drink and celebrate?" She said, "But we don't have any booze!" I nodded agreement as we had not brought a bottle. Then it dawned on me. "The hell we don't! We got a trunk full!"

We pulled over the side of the road, got us a dang bottle of bourbon, fixed ourselves a drink. What's funny about this all is that we didn't get back to Goodland until five or six that afternoon, and there was one poor guy—Jack Robins—who'd sat there all afternoon at the bar waiting for us to get back. We were so happy with him sitting there waiting that we just bought all of his drinks! That's a true story, and we had a ball.

≈ 12 ≈

TRYING TO MAKE IT UPSTAIRS

Al Repstorf, was the greatest banker that ever lived. He had started a bank for the Mackle brothers on Marco that was the fifth fastest growing bank in the state of Florida—the First Bank of Marco Island. Al believed we couldn't miss with the upstairs bar.

He said, "You got all these windows around up here and these docks down below, and people can come and sit up here, have a drink, talk about their boats, overlook Goodland. It's gonna work. This is beautiful!"

Well, it never worked. People wouldn't *stay* up there. I don't know why. They would have a drink, maybe two, then leave. The upstairs just did not work.

Now downstairs, all they had to do was get outta the boat, come in the back door of the bar, and they'd sit in there all afternoon. They had a pool table and a juke box, so they had something to do. So we're going broke with that upstairs bar. We'd been up there about a month, and we had no business, and it just wasn't going right.

So we hired a piano player, Alan Bogdan, a well-known entertainer on Marco. He had a big book of songs, and he could play anything in there. So I started singing old songs from Perry Como, Bing Crosby, Frank Sinatra with Alan Bogdan.

We started doing that in the late summer months upstairs. He had a piano and a keyboard and could play them both at once. I was singing and it was going along pretty good. We were getting a crowd, even in the summer. As we got into the fall, the crowd started picking up a little better and Alan, the son-of-a-gun, *quit* and started grouper fishing—with *those* hands. So that ruined *that* little show.

To keep things going we come up with the idea of having a Gong Show. I hung two great big pots on the wall over a booth, and we had a little stage up there. I had two couples sitting up there with big, *big* pot spoons. Anyone who wanted to perform got a microphone and would sing or tell a joke or dance. I think we awarded the winner 10 bucks.

Oh, they'd beat on them pots and pans like crazy. It was so funny. That lasted a total of six weeks. We ran completely out of talent whatsoever. I even wrote a poem for Steve about growing up. He was only about 8 years old, and he recited this poem and won the "Gong Show" that night. I never will forget it, my little youngest son.

Eight days after I got the liquor license, they changed the law to 150 seats, and I'd have never had to go to war like I did to get it. The new law said you had to park 75 cars, have 400-plus square feet and 150 people.

Around this time, Lexie Herron had come back down, and he said, "Well, boy, whadda ya wanna do?"

I said, "Well, Lex, I want you to build me a bar downstairs. Having the bar upstairs is just not working."

He said, "Alright, boy, I'll start Monday."

He built the bar, he put the shelves in for the liquor, we put the freezer back in there so we'd have a freezer for the beer mugs, just like we had it before. We got two pool tables on consignment, and a jukebox.

I went to Sears—this is how broke I was—I charged a TV for $400.

I told Lex, "I don't know *when* I'll be able to pay you." He said, "Boy, you pay me when you can."

He started rebuilding the bar on Monday, and on Thursday afternoon, he picked up his tools and said, "Well, you got it, boy," and we opened the doors and were back in the bar business.

In 30 days, I paid the Sears TV off, paid Lexie, and we were back making money.

Downstairs, people started coming in like crazy. Faye was working the bar, and she didn't like it. She's smart, and she catches on quick. She had a bar-book, and if you wanted a Rusty Nail, well, she'd read it up in the book and fix it for you.

So then comes, God bless her heart, Fran Pack and her husband, Dennis. And Fran's still with me today. She's the longest-running employee, other than my family. She's been with me 27 years.

So, one day, Fran and Dennis come in the bar. Dennis was a crane operator on Marco Island. He worked every day building Marco with that big crane over there. I was behind the bar, because I helped when I could.

Dennis said to me, country-like, "My wife's a barmaid."

I said, "Really?"

"And she's lookin' for a job," he said.

I turned to Fran and said, "You know how to mix all them drinks?"

She said, "Yeah, I worked in LaBelle at the Long Branch Saloon for 12 years!"

I said, "Faye, this lady here works a bar and she's lookin' for a job."

She said, "Well, hell, hire her *now!*"

So I did, and she came to work the next day and has been with me ever since. She's a good person too. Honest. I trust her with the place.

Dennis worked construction on Marco, so he started telling his work buddies where his wife was working, so they all started coming over to the bar, and we got business! We got construction workers running every which way.

We started just using the upstairs for occasional private parties or Christmas parties, and that's exactly the way it is today. You can go up there and watch a football game on Sundays and stuff like that.

≈ 13 ≈

FIRES!

Stan's caught fire twice. Both times, our neighbors saved us by spotting the fires before the place burnt to the ground.

The first time we caught fire, Faye and I and the three boys were living upstairs in the little apartment. (This is one time where an alcoholic absolutely saved our whole place!)

A guy next door leased the bait shop, and he was a mechanic who sold shrimp and fishing stuff. He drank a lot. I don't know if he ever slept, but this one particular morning he was up at four in the morning working on an outboard motor.

Meanwhile, one of my waitresses had a coffee pot out in the dining room next to the window where a curtain was, and she'd left it on. So about 3:30 or 3:45 a.m., the wire got so hot on that coffee pot, it just blew. When it did, it caught that curtain on fire, and it caught the ceiling on fire, and it was in the dining room.

So my neighbor was over there working on this boat, and he saw the flames and the smoke, and he got in my back door somehow or other. It woke the kid up who was washing dishes for me—he was living on a houseboat out there, and he had a key to get in. So they got in and were trying to put the fire out, not waking us up.

All of a sudden I heard all this noise down in my restaurant, and I said, "Dang, somebody's breakin' in the restaurant, Faye!" and I had to go find out what the hell was going on. So I went outside and went over to the roof and looked down, and I see this guy stooped down doing something out there.

I yelled, "What the hell you doin' down there? You breakin' in my place?! Whadda you doin'?"

And he looked up, he said, "No Stan! It's Whitey, your place is on fire!"

I said, "Holy God!"

I come running out of there—I hate to say this, but I had on baby blue silk pajamas. I came down those steps and went running in there. The flames were everywhere—smoke and everything.

I went in the back door of the kitchen and said, "Gimme some water, Chuck!" So he runs to the sink and gets a little pan of water, and I said, "Oh my God, no . . ." and I said "Stay right here, I gotta cut the power to the building!" I knew what I had to do. Adrenaline was working, so I ran to the back and pulled the main switch on the building, and then I hollered at the guy, "Throw that fish hose in!" This was a hose we used to clean fish. Thank God it was long enough that it could reach the kitchen and then the dining room.

So I got up there and I just put the fire out. It was already in the rafters. It had burnt the ceiling, and a spot about four or five feet wide fell down, and the rafters were on fire. It was fixin' to *go* man, I tell ya!

I put that fire out, and I looked around. It was daylight, and I was smutty all over, I've still got on my pajamas, I don't even realize it. But I got the fire out. So I said, "Faye go on up there and get me some jeans, and a shirt, and I'll go back there and change." So she did, and I had some spare towels, and I told my two kids, "Now listen, guys. You guys are not goin' to school today. We open at 11 a.m. We gotta get this place cleaned up."

Every place in the dining room was smutty. Any place that there was a cobweb that you couldn't see before, you could now see it because of the soot. All the dishes, knives, forks and glasses were sooty.

I said, "You kids go in there and wash all the dishes, and give me

At age 15 I wanted to be a singer.

*At age 17, singing at City Hall
Auditorium, Bessemer, Alabama.*

*On the same stage in Bessemer
some 50 years later.*

New Caledonia in the Pacific. I'm shirtless in front.

I joined the Navy in 1944.

New Caledonia, 1945.

In 1962 my campaign photo, running for 2nd VP, Communication Workers of America, Local #3107 in Miami. I came in second.

With Faye, Easter Sunday 1957 at our home in Hialeah, Florida.

Fishing on Marco Island in the 60s. Life was good.

My favorite little convertible in Hialeah, Florida. Russ is standing up through the roof.

The three Gober brothers at family reunion. To my left is Wally and then Colonel Butch.

Mullet Festival 1987 and the Back Porch Band.

*King Buzzard Stan in 1985 awarding
the first Mullet Festival trophy to
Lora Britton from Isle of Capri.*

*With Brenda Byers at the Marco Beach
Hotel, Caxambas Lounge. Singing with
her and The Neighbors Four band.*

*My brother, Colonel Butch, at
the bar on a recent visit.*

Having a sociable drink with Bill Rose.

*My very good friend Lexie Herron. We had
been fishing. He always called me "boy."*

Playing a pirate on Halloween at Stan's.

On stage with Larry Scheetz at one
of many Hospice fund-raisers.

Henry Watkins Sr., owner of Naples
Beach & Golf Club. He loved Stan's,
came every Sunday by boat.

A great woman with a great heart, my
good friend Donna Hazle Hanzman,
Mrs. All American, 2003.

A private consultation about the
Buzzard Lope with some fans.

Getting ready with special
instructions from Queen Mary.

The end of the buzzard dance.

My mother with her dogwood tree
in Bessemer, Alabama.

My younger
brother—we called
him Butch—won
many medals
in Vietnam.

Takes New Command in Viet Nam

Major Floyd C. Gober of Huntsville, Viet Nam, is shown with Major
who recently assumed command of Matorson, left, and Lt. Col. Jones, the
the 334th Armed Helicopter Co. in battalion commander.

Butch takes command.

Awarding Boyd Wiles a medallion as member
of the Greatest Generation. Boyd hit the beach
at Normandy on D-Day June 6, 1944.

My hippie buddy Kevin Thomas, my
main man for almost 20 years.

With Joe Klimas and Ken Venturi,
supporting a cancer benefit in memory
of Faye, upstairs at Stan's.

Celebrating my 65th birthday. I made a talk and gave all 3 sons a key to the restaurant. I told them I was through. I lied.

With good friends Bob and Pat Flagg from St. Louis and Marco celebrating 4th July 1997.

With Anna. She inspired me to do the patio and start the Mullet Festival.

Two of Anna's models promoting the Island Woman Boutique.

With daughter Becky on one of her visits to me from Seattle. Great time. I love her dearly.

The Cartwright gang. Left to right: Steve, Jay, Stan and Russ, at one of the parties in memory of Faye.

Buddy Harrison and his wife Bobby.
Great friends and supporters of Stan's.

Captain Catfish looking macho.

Good friend Cindy Anderson. Without
her this book would never have been.

Faye in relaxing moment in the 70s on our boat.

My first boat at the Dinner Key
Marina, Miami with Faye,
Russ and Jay going fishing.

Doing Buzzard Lope first time, 1985.

*Signing my first 45 recording,
February 1985.*

With good friends Whitey and Fuzzy Thurston.

My good friend Bobby Gideon.

With good friends Joe Patava and Kitty Noom.

With good friends Joe and Barbara Klimas.

*With Larry and Kathy Scheetz
for a hospice auction.*

With Norm and Debbie, the Hot Damn Duo, from Maine. They play at Stan's in the winter.

Celebrating New Year's Eve with Lynn.

The Buzzard Boat Float. Lots of fun.

Pete and Wayne, entertainers all around the U.S. and especially at Sloppy Joe's in Key West. And my super waitress, Bonnie.

Great friend and entertainer all around Marco, Mitch Peters and wife Lora.

July 4, 1985 — Goodland barbecue and parade organized by the late Betty Bruno, myself and other good citizens of Goodland. With me pulling the Buzzard Boat Float are County Commissioner John Pistor and his wife Alice.

A painting of Stan in the Van Liebig Art Center in Naples.

Good friend Roger Raymond and the Morningstar Show Band.

Son Steve barbequing ribs for the 4th of July parade, 1985.

With Steve, my manager at Stan's.

Canadian friends Charles Bennet "The Bear" and Kerri. I named them Honorary Americans. They support us in every way. They give like Americans.

As a top salesman and installer of new phones in Miami. I received the small phone/pen set. My manager got the big trophy for doing such a good job of managing me. That was the first time I met him.

*Good friends Ken Venturi and
wife Beau. Beau is buried next
to Faye at Marco Cemetery.*

*Lynn with Jeff and Terri Walker,
our Nashville connection.*

*With brother Wally in Oatman,
California on Route 66, summer 2005.*

*With Larry Scheetz, a fund-
raiser for Wishing Well.*

*At the World War II Memorial,
Washington, D.C.*

*My 79th birthday party at Sloppy
Joe's in Key West, 2005, with good
friends and my help at Stan's.*

Lynn and Kittie manning food booth
at our 1st Hospice Benefit in 1995.

Left to right: The late Betty Bruno, honorary
mayor of Goodland, myself, and Fran my faithful
employee for 28 years and still going strong.

Son Russ and his wife Joanne who
has been working for us for over 30
years and still going strong.

With my good friend Chuck Alexander,
a Naples businessman. He built the
first chickee bar in Naples.

Don Riddles and Jeff Hilt playing at Stan's.

Singing with my buddy Alan
Sandlin, a long time friend.

My good friend Johnny Angel singing
at a Hospice benefit at Stan's.

Fishing with Elinor Smalley. I preached her husband's
funeral at Stan's. Chuck Smalley was a great guy.

The late great Jack Hamburg, a terrific
joke teller and impressive Uncle Sam.

With Father Pat Boyhan, a wonderful
friend always helpful with any benefits.

Mike Ditka, the great Chicago Bears
player, coach and super bowl winner, helped
us with the Wishing Well benefit.

With girlfriend Lynn in Nashville having
fun on the General Jackson paddle wheeler.

*With brother Wally having a beer
in Arizona, summer 2005.*

*My favorite County Commissioner,
Donna Fiala, truly a great friend.*

*With Lynn, Debbie Boehner, and Barbara
Humbrackt. Having fun at Stan's Bar.*

*Left to right: Smitty, Liz, myself, son
Russ at the bar enjoying a cocktail.*

*With my friend Hugh who flies down
every year from New Jersey for my
Key West birthday party trip.*

PROCLAMATION

WHEREAS,   in Goodland, Florida, there exists a well-known restaurant called "Stan's Idle Hour Seafood Restaurant" ("Stan's"); and,

WHEREAS,   at Stan's, patrons engage in an activity that can loosely be described as a "dance" known far and wide as the "Buzzard's Lope"; and,

WHEREAS,   in keeping with the spirit of the widely renowned "Buzzard's Lope," the Board of County Commissioners ("Board") has been requested to name as "Buzzards' Bay South" that small saltwater inlet north of and adjacent to Stan's; and,

WHEREAS,   after due deliberations, the Board has decided to name the subject small saltwater inlet "Buzzards Bay South"; and,

WHEREAS,   there exists in Cape Cod Bay, Massachusetts, a larger body of saltwater called "Buzzards Bay," which should not be confused with "Buzzards' Bay South" of Goodland, Florida.

NOW THEREFORE, be it proclaimed by the Board of County Commissioners of Collier County, Florida, that:

1. The small saltwater inlet north of and adjacent to "Stan's Idle Hour Seafood Restaurant," 221 Goodland Drive West, Goodland, Florida, never previously having been named by Collier County, nor insofar as we have been able to ascertain, by the Government of the United States, the National Oceanographic and Atmospheric Administration, the State of Florida or any other governmental entity having jurisdiction is hereafter to be known locally as "Buzzards' Bay South."

2. The small saltwater inlet to be known locally as "Buzzards' Bay South" is located at approximately Latitude 25 degrees, 55 minutes, 33 seconds North; and Longitude 81 degrees, 38 minutes, 54 seconds West.

DONE AND ORDERED THIS 14th Day of December, 1999.

BOARD OF COUNTY COMMISSIONERS
COLLIER COUNTY, FLORIDA

PAMELA S. MAC'KIE, CHAIRWOMAN

ATTEST:

DWIGHT E. BROCK, CLERK

I was pleased when the Collier County Commissioners honored us with the above proclamation in December 1999 naming Buzzard Bay South.

Shirley Lewandowski, my girl friend
Lynn's mother. She passed away on
March 15, 2005. God bless her.

Son Steve and his girl friend Trish.

Larry and Barbara Humbrackt, my
mixed marriage friends. He's from
Chicago and she's from Alabama.

Son Jay and his wife Caren.

Singing at the lighting of the Christmas Tree
at Town Center on Marco Island with my
accompanist Jeff Hilt, December 2005. And
we left Christmas in the Christmas tree.

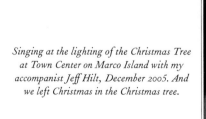

some cleanin' fluid and I'll clean the dining room up." I put a rug over a burnt hole in the carpet, and I just took the rest of the burnt curtain down.

We opened right on time at 11 a.m. like nothing had ever happened. Maybe two or three people came in that day, but they said, "Dang! Smells like something's burnin' or there was a fire or somethin'." I said, "Ya."

But I wasn't tellin'! I didn't dare call the fire department or anybody because I knew my insurance would double or go up or whatever the hell. So we just did it ourselves.

That was a blessing that our neighbor was out there working on that motor. Otherwise we could have been burnt to the ground.

The other time we caught fire was due to a butane tank. We had a little chickee hut and a grill at the back of the building where we did the ribs every Sunday before we put in the outdoor show.

I had a regular guy to do the grilling every Sunday, but he couldn't do it one day, and we got another guy, a customer, to do it. He was an alright guy.

So he's got to get started at 8 a.m. so the ribs would be ready by noon. We were using a butane tank that had a little ⅜″ copper line that goes to the grill, and it was sitting over to the side of it. It was a tall tank, not one of those little ones.

This guy decided he's got the grill on, and he wants a cup of coffee. So he goes down to what was then the Goodland Bay Marina and gets him a coffee and leaves the grill on. For some reason or another, the line going to the grill came loose.

The neighbor across the water saw the flames, and she described it like this: "When that copper wire came loose on the end of the grill, it was sprayin' fire like a flame thrower!"

It sprayed the fire over there and caught the chickee on fire. It had the patio burning in about three places and it was coming into the corner of the building too!

So, again, unbeknownst to me, I'm down here at the house, two and a half blocks away still asleep, and they call the fire department. I hear the fire department and I wonder, "What in the world is that?" But then I got the call that my place was on fire!

I went down there, and, boy, the fire department is tearin' my place up. They start knocking windows out, knocking the roof in. The grill was right by the store room, it wasn't even close to the kitchen or the dining room or the front counter. So actually, they put it out, but I had to replace some ceiling work there and I had to replace a window, and some tiles on the side of the building.

That was a close call. Thank God my neighbor across the water saw it from her kitchen window. Thank God for my neighbors.

≈ 14 ≈

DRUNKS ARE LIKE LITTLE CHILDREN

I never was a tough guy, but I don't put up with customers not respecting my family and anybody else around me. I want to give you good service, I'll help you, I'll do anything for you, but, by God, you gotta respect my family and what we're doing here.

I found out one thing about running a bar business: Drunks are like little children. If you just get them over that drunk night, usually everything's fine.

The Boudreaux Brothers

There were three Boudreaux brothers, French-Canadian construction workers. They were all about 6′1″ and wore cowboy boots and cowboy hats. They gave me a bad time every now and then.

Before Faye and I even got the bar opened inside, those brothers came in one night. They started out at the coffee counter. I had a big, beautiful polished turtle shell there.

This Boudreaux boy said to his friend, "Go ahead and take that if you want it," and I heard it. I went around behind the counter, and he was at the front door, and I said, "By God, you ain't takin' nothin' outta here!" And I made the mistake of pushing him at the door. Well it was like pushing on a wall. He didn't move. When he didn't move, I thought, "Oh my gosh!" Just about that time, my son, Russ, who was just 16, but he was like six foot tall, he jumped up right quick and got in the middle of us because the guy was about to hit me.

Russ said, "Don't you hit my dad, I'll kill you!"

And the guy, just like a little kid said, "Well, tell him to quit pushin' me!"

I never knew where we stood with those Boudreaux boys or what they were going to do when they were around. It was an uneasy situation. We loaned them money once upon a time. We always tried to help the guys who were working around there when we could, let them have a little credit for the food and stuff.

Time goes by, and they're still around. We're keeping our cool. We haven't been in any fights with them. I'd tell them, "We're not gonna have any fightin' around here, this is a restaurant and we come to give you service. We're not gonna take nothin' off of ya."

One of the brothers owed us money, so time goes by and we got the bar open. (This was before Fran came to work for us.) Now one of the guys came in the bar one night with another guy, and Faye and I are behind the bar. The guy had two 16-ounce beers, one in each hand, and I said, "Hey, man, don't bring your beer in here. We *sell* beer." Well, Faye spoke up. She'd learned to be outspoken with them and she wouldn't take nothing off of them.

She said, "Yeah, and if you ain't got our money, you can get the hell outta here!"

Well, now, I'm the husband, and they're looking at me, and I'm thinking "I gotta say *somethin'!*" So I said, "Yeah, that goes for me too!"

So now the Boudreaux Brother, he was the tall one, he said, "You little no good mother-punk, you!" He said, "You come outside and I'll beat the hell outta you!"

Well, I know what it means to lose your mind, because I lost my mind right then. I kicked the back door of the bar open, and went into the store room where I had a little 410 shotgun over the door on two nails up there. I reached and got it, brought it down.

Everybody in the bar—there was about four or five sitting there—they saw the expression on my face, and they laid down. They got outta the way. I came around with that shotgun, and those two guys hit the door, *runnin'!*

By the time I got to the front door, they had that old Ford they were driving backed out and just puttin' it in forward, and boy, they were scratchin' grass and weeds and shells and stuff 'cause we didn't have blacktop.

When they went down a little bit further, the one on the passenger side was just turned white and I remember seeing him try to get down because I had the shotgun pointing at them. I blasted the side of the car with that shotgun, and when I did, it woke me up!

I said to myself, "Oh my God . . . Hell, I'm bad as they are! What in the hell are you doin'? You crazy?!"

But I figured that they might come back and try to hurt me, because I'd made a drastic move here, so I went upstairs. We lived in a little apartment upstairs. The whole upstairs had a big concrete wall around it about two feet high around the top of the roof. I sat up there for about two hours with the shotgun, thinking if they come back, I'm gonna challenge them. I'm gonna tell 'em "Don't mess with me!" Now, you know, I'm premeditated. I'm thinking things through because I know I was acting crazy shooting the shotgun.

Those boys go on back to Marco, and they ran into Russ the next day. They said, "Russ, you tell your dad we could have him put in jail for shootin' at us."

And he said, "Well, I'll tell ya, my dad's sick of you guys. He's had enough of you guys."

They said, "Well you tell him we ain't *never* comin' back over there again!" And they didn't. I don't know where they went.

Two years went by. One night I was sitting there at the end of the bar, and Fran was working then, behind the bar, and here came one of the Boudreaux brothers with another guy. They walked in and I said, "Fran come here, quick," and she came over.

I said, "That's one of the brothers I shot with that shotgun." Russ was in there cooking, and I told Fran, "If anything happens to me, you go back there and get Russ quick."

I wasn't going to get up. I was scared, but I wasn't going to get up and let them think that I was. So I was sitting at the end of the bar, and they order two beers, and this guy takes a drink. He looks down at the end of that bar and sees *me*, and he put the beer down and he come right down where I was.

He looked at me dead in the eyes and he said, "Do you remember shootin' my brother with that shotgun?"

I said, "Yeah, I do."

And that son-of-a-gun grabbed me, and he put the biggest bear hug on me you ever seen! And he said, "Them were the good ol' days, wasn't it?"

I said to him, "Well, they might have been for *you*, but I was scared shitless, myself!"

Then we laughed about it, and I've never seen him since. Never.

Crazy Don

There are a few little things that are a little hazardous about running a bar business. One I remember very well. When we got liquor and we opened up "Stan's Bar," there were two or three of us sitting there— one was a young man, one was a couple—and a young fellow that I'd seen around town, by the name of Don came in.

Don was about 5'9" and probably weighed about 170 pounds. He was just drifting through town. I didn't know him that well, but I knew of him as he'd been around for a few months and come in on a few occasions when he had a little bit of money.

So here he was drinking in the bar upstairs. He was acting up a little bit, then he went on downstairs.

I said, "Well, where'd that guy go?"

"I don't know, he left," somebody said.

I went and looked out the window, and he was standing in the middle of the street. He had long hair like a hippie, and he had on combat boots. Now we're watching him from upstairs. He took his boots off, standing in the middle of the street, and he threw them across the street towards the motel. He started yelling at God, up in the air, cussin' and raisin' hell, shakin' his hair and everything like that. Now I'm thinking he's crazy.

He disappeared under the awning. Under the awning there was a pay phone. Now I don't know what he was doing. So, as it turns out, unbeknownst to me, he called the police and told them there was a fight at Stan's. Then he came back upstairs, and I was sitting there at the bar. He sat down, then after a little bit he turned to me and said, "Your family's gonna hate me for what I'm gonna do to you."

I said, "What's that, Don?"

He said, "I'm gonna kill you."

I said, "You gotta be kiddin' me."

He said, "No, I'm gonna kill you in about two minutes."

I said, "Listen, man, quit talkin' to me like that. You're makin' me nervous. Cut that bullshit out!"

He said, "I really mean it."

I said, "Well, I'll tell you what, I'm gonna get somebody up here to get you outta here!"

So I reached for the phone, and when I picked it up, my wife was already on the phone downstairs, and she said, "Stan, there's two cops here. They explained they got a call that there's a fight here."

I said, "Well there may be. Not a fight, but this damn Don up here says he's gonna kill me, and I want you to send Russ up here."

So my son Russ came up. He's a big guy by that point, weighing over 200 pounds. He walked up to Don and said, "Don, what the hell's the matter with you, boy?" And he reached up and lightly slapped him on the cheek. When he did that, that boy come off that barstool and dove into Russ like a football player and knocked him over one table into *another* table.

Now they're on the ground scuffling, and I jumped up and went over there and hit him with a karate chop as hard as I could on the back of his neck and it didn't even phase him. About that time, Faye heard all the noise of the table collapsing upstairs, so she sent those cops up.

In the meantime, a young man at the bar came over and was trying to help hold Don. He was like a damn stuck pig, you couldn't hold him. He was wild, he was just crazy. So the cops finally got him, and it took a little struggle to get him turned face down so they could handcuff him.

They finally got him handcuffed, and he was kicking and carrying on. They were dragging him. They said, "You goin' down these stairs, whether you like it or not!" He kicked and screamed and yelled all the way down those stairs.

They got him in the cop car, and he tore the back seat all up. So they got him up there in Naples, and they made the mistake of taking the handcuffs off. When they did, he went crazy. There was a young police guy I knew who was a black belt up there, and he turned him ever'which way but loose and damn near killed him. Then they got him in the cell.

We went to court. The only reason he was in court was that he resisted arrest and did damage to the cop car. The story they gave me was that "As far as him sayin' he was gonna kill you, that's no charge, 'cause we can't charge him for sayin' that. Only way we can charge him is if he *does* it."

I said, "Oh, isn't that beautiful?!"

So there he is in court sitting over there wearing a Stan's T-shirt, and he's smilin' and wavin' at me during the trial. They give him three months, and I prayed to God that he'd never come back. Thank God I never saw him again.

Couples Only

In the dining room, we're just not making it. It's the summer and we just don't have much business. But a guy came in there with a four-piece country band. He was a Christian guy—not at all a hard-core kind of guy. We put them in the end of the dining room and built a little plywood stage for them to stand on, and I put a sign on the door that read "Couples Only."

Well, one night, here came four construction workers, and they went straight into the Couples Only dining room. Faye came and told me there's four of these construction workers out there in amongst the couples only.

So I went out there, and I said, "Fellas, you guys can't stay out here, it's couples only. You can come out here at the counter with me." I said, "You can hear the music, but you won't be disrupting some guy and his wife or girlfriend."

One spoke up, "Well, hell, what's the matter with you? Ah, you're crazy, we ain't doin' nothin'!"

I said, "Well, I know, but I don't want no trouble."

They said, "That's the way you feel?"

I said, "Yeah, c'mon out to the counter."

Well, I argued with them a little bit, and they said, "Ah, hell. We'll go over to the Snake Pit."

The Snake Pit was the ideal fish camp over in Caxambas, which the Mackle brothers did not own, and it was right in the middle of Caxambas, over by the clam docks. It was four wooden houses, and they put a bar and a pool table in the biggest one. That's where all the really rough ones would go because it was a rough place. Everything went. Anything went.

The deputy sheriff assigned to Marco liked the Snake Pit. Les Binns was the only law enforcement we had back then. Everybody knew him.

He loved it because he knew where all the troublemakers were. If he ever really had a problem with them, he'd get somebody from Naples to come down with him, but he got along good with everybody. He was one of those kinda guys that was the law, but he would take some of the drunks home rather than lock them up. He would lean a lot and everybody loved Les Binns.

So these four construction workers said, "To hell with you, we'll go to the Snake Pit."

I thought they'd left. Our kids were little, and they were up in the apartment upstairs. They called down for me to bring them some food. I fixed them something to eat and took it up to them. When I came back out of the apartment, I heard some people downstairs sort of *rumbling*. I thought, "What is that?"

I walked over to the back of the roof and looked down, and there were those four guys bitchin' about me! They were saying stuff like, "I bet he owns ever' one of these boats out here. We oughta sink ever' damn one of 'em, that's what we oughta do!" Then one of 'em said, "Well, he's probably already called the law."

And I shouted down, "Aw, the hell I ain't yet, but by God, I'm fixin' to! You guys get the hell outta here and I mean it!"

They yelled back, "You come off of that roof and we'll whip the hell outta ya!"

I said, "Meet me around them stairs! I got my damn gun with me and I ain't takin' no crap off of you guys!"

Well, when I said that, they came around the building, and I ain't *fixin'* to go down those steps! I got no gun up there with me because it's down in the restaurant. I was just bluffing them.

So they start goin' toward the Little Bar, which was just a wooden building, not a cement one like it is now. They were bitching and hollering at me, but they're movin' on all the time and I'm yelling at them. So when they get on out of the way, I go back down into the restaurant.

All of a sudden Faye said, "Stan, I wish you'd look at them four construction guys. They're over there, across the street sitting down in the weeds." And there they were stooped down in the high weeds there with a six-pack of beer, looking at the restaurant.

I said to Faye, "What in the hell do you think they're doin' over there?" She said, "Waitin' on you to come out, or close I guess."

I thought, "Oh, boy."

So a guy who called himself Denver came in from Little Bar and said with a slur, "Whadda-them-guys-doin-cross-th-street?"

Faye said, "They're waitin' on Stan. I guess they want to beat him up."

I said, "You know what, Denver? I'm gonna give them SOBs a chance to beat my ass. I'm gonna go out there right now. But I gotta damn gun here, loaded six times, and if they mess with me, I'm gonna shoot ever' damn one of 'em!"

They didn't know I really wouldn't. So I went out the front door, without the gun. I walked around a car that was parked there, so that put me pretty far out toward the road. I walked around the car and down to where the Boutique is now (it was a bait shop back then). I walked all around like I was looking for something. Well, nothing happened, so I walked all the way back. They never said a word to me. They looked at me, but they didn't say anything.

So I went back in and told Denver, "Denver, you know what? You go over there and you tell them damn guys that I've had enough of them damn aggravatin' me and if they mess with me I'm gonna shoot 'em."

He said, "By-god-I-didn't-come-in-here-ta-hear-this-kinda-shit! All-I-come-in-here-for-waza-beer-an-I-don'need-this-crap!"

So he went out the door, and he goes right over there! Now I don't know what he said, but when he was through, they all got up and they went back to the Little Bar!

I was 44 or 45, still spunky as hell. And I just had to do it. I went out the back door and went around the restaurant and I watched where they went. They went up to the Little Bar and were standing out front. I snuck right up to the end of the building where I could hear and see them. I peeked around and they was cussin' me—saying everything they think of me, just drinkin' and cussin'!

I started laughing at them in my heart, because it tickled me what they were saying about me. I had to get the hell out of there before they heard me laughing at 'em. I came back, and Faye said, "What are you laughin' at?" and I said, "They up there cussing me, with ever'thang they can think of!"

A couple of days go by, and two of them came to the coffee counter to get something to eat. I went around the counter where they were and grabbed both of them around the shoulders.

I said, "What the hell you guys trying to do to me the other night?! Was you tryin' to get my goat or what?!"

They looked at me and they said, "Oh man, you know what? We was just drunk, we don't know what the hell, we didn't mean nothin' by it!"

And that's the way that went. I praise the Lord for giving me the knack of being able to do that and make them see that I wasn't mad or holding anything against them. And they never gave me any more trouble.

Now that was the construction guys on Marco. But it helped me that they were coming in more and more every week for months building Marco. They started working around the clock to get Marco finished and to get the sales up.

They were comin' in all the time, but when I shot at the one set, that made a believer out of all of them. The ones I shot at went over to Marco and said, "Now don't *mess* with that guy, he must be crazy!"

The New Jersey Strangers

In the bar one afternoon, there were two construction workers from New Jersey. One of them was married. They were just run-of-the-mill iron workers. The gal was drunk and kept knocking over drinks, and she knocked over a barstool, and she was just interfering with the guys playing pool. And I told the guy, "You've got to contain her, man, she's just disrupting the bar." I think it was a Sunday afternoon.

She kept on acting up and messing up and so I finally said, "Listen, if you can't do nothin' with her, then I'm gonna get someone over here that can!"

And the tallest guy looked me dead in the eye and said, "Well I'll tell you one thang. We ain't gonna get no better!" And he put his hand out to shake my hand.

Now I'm behind the bar. I thought he was gonna try to yank me over that bar, so I braced myself as I reached my hand out, and he squeezed my hand as he said, "So I guess we'd better leave."

And they left.

The next week, they went to a bar up a ways in Collier County. They were sitting at the bar—so the story went—and the guy told his best buddy, "I'm in love with your wife." And she said, "And I'm in love with him."

So the guy sat there and took it, according to the story I was told. So his wife and his best buddy went to the restroom. When they got back there in the restrooms, the other fella got up, followed them back there, went in the latrine and shot her on the commode and him too.

The bartender ran back there, and the guy shot the bartender in the shoulder and then killed himself.

And I'm messing with these folks?!

I'm thinking the Lord is looking after me. And I totally believe that part of the Bible where it says, "If you keep my commandments, I will direct your path." And He always has directed my path, because I'm not the smartest guy in the world.

But things come to me to do. I don't know where the hell they come from. I don't sit there and figure it out, like the songs.

≈ 15 ≈

"STAN, PLEASE GO TO SLEEP"

I've always wanted to sing and entertain, and that's what I did growing up in Alabama. I never was really a country singer, although I like that kind of music.

Oh, the songs just come to me. I've sat down and *tried* to make myself write a song. But they just have to come to me. If I start singing it in the truck or something, then it's *there*! Then I put it on a tape recorder as quick as I can to remember it. And I've forgotten some because I didn't.

Sometimes I'll be goin' to Naples in the truck and all of a sudden I'm singing a whole song that comes to me, melody and all.

I wanted to be a singer all my little life. When I was about 9 years old, I used to try to mimic Bing Crosby when he would come on the radio, on the Kraft Music Hall on Wednesday nights. We had one of those old radios. It had the dog sitting there looking into the megaphone. Bing would come on, and no matter what I was doing, like most kids that were outside running and jumping and playing hide and go seek, I'd be in the house and just slide right on the floor and just lay there and hear the Bing sing. He inspired me to want to be a singer.

I'd lay in the bed at night and try to sing what I remembered of Bing

Crosby. Mother would say, "Stan, please go to sleep; let us get some sleep!"

I'd be singin' out loud. My voice would be crackin' and poppin' y'know. Songs like, "Moonlight Becomes You," "Pennies from Heaven." I'd sing, *Every time it rains, it rains pennies from heaven. Don't you know each cloud contains pennies from heaven.*

Another would sound like this, *Kiss me once, and kiss me twice and kiss me once again . . . been a long, long time.* So mom would say, "Go to sleep, will ya?"

In high school, I met a young man who played the piano. He was from a pretty well-off family, and we didn't have anything. We kinda rehearsed a little bit. I did a couple of plays in school.

I kept on singing where I could, in the Navy, in Miami, right up until we got to Goodland. Then I started working so hard on the motel and restaurant, throughout the '70s, I had no music in me.

It was after Faye died that I met Brenda Byers, who was on the circuit all around the country doing shows with a band at hotels. She ate at our place and I got to know her. We used to go catch her show.

I told her one day that I sang and had songs in my head, and she said, "Well, whadda ya got?" and I sang "I Left My Heart in Downtown Goodland." I also had "What Kind of Fish Is That?" which Frankie DeLonzo from New Jersey helped me write.

Well, she invited me over to the Marco Beach Hotel one Saturday. It was in the Caxambas Lounge. She said she'd get the band and we'd record those two songs. I sang "Downtown Goodland" fairly well because singing slow ballads is my bag, but when we got to "What Kind of Fish Is That?" well, it was a little bit of a skippy thing. It had a lot of words in it, and man, I just couldn't get the timing down.

So finally, Brenda got Bart, her lead singer, to sing it, just for the tape. After that, I got hooked up with a guy over there in Fort Lauderdale who was in the record business, and I got him to stamp out some 45s. The least he would do was 300. So I got 300 45 rpm records of me singing "I Left My Heart in Downtown Goodland," and Bart singing "What Kind of Fish Is That?"

"What Kind of Fish Is That?"

About when Faye was in the hospital with cancer, I was getting back into music and songs were whirling around in my head—I had written six back in Miami. Now all of a sudden I'm cleaning fish for the restaurant, and I keep hearing people keep ask me "What kind of fish is that?" "What kind of fish is *that*?"

It kept rolling around in my head. "What kind of fish is that, where'd you catch him at?" and all that stuff. And that's when a lady got her nephew down from New Jersey, and he played guitar and was a sharp guy. He took my words and he said he'd help me. I told him I had this song in my head but I really couldn't put it together.

I said, "I don't know what it is. I can't get a bridge for the song." The bridge is the middle part. You got your melody, and you got the bridge that comes back to the melody.

He said, "Lemme take it." So he went to Northville, New Jersey, to put that song together with his brother-in-law and when he sent it back down to Goodland, he actually put the melody to it and everything. I didn't have the right melody. I just couldn't get it in my head. I changed two lines in it and recorded it, and it's a pretty good little song.

The Blue Ridge Publishing Company took that song but only for a year. So that contract expired without anyone picking it up, and that's about as close as I came to getting the songs published.

"I Left My Heart in Downtown Goodland"

One night, me and a group of people were up in the "skyroom." It was over the cistern which used to hold all the water for Goodland.

Some gals, some co-eds from Chicago were up there and they were singing and carrying on. I got up there and was singing with them. One of them said, "Can you sing, 'I Left My Heart in San Francisco'?"

I said, "Yeah! I left my heart ..." and before I could sing anymore, they sang, " ... in downtown Goodland!" And I said, "My God! That's kinda crazy."

They left and I went in the back, sat in the dining room and put all the words that's on my tape: *I left my heart in downtown Goodland, under the bridge, it's home to me ... when I come home to her, she's gonna kill me, 'cause this is not my wife you see.*

And I sang that one night over there at the Marco Beach Hotel with Brenda Byers, the gal that got me to do the first two songs with her band and taped it for me. Brenda's still singing today. She's been in Vegas, she's been on George Burns' TV show. She's just one step down from being one of the top notches, but she goes all over the country singing.

A bunch of insurance convention people were staying at the Marco Beach Hotel, and Brenda called me out of the audience to sing "I Left My Heart in Downtown Goodland." Russ and his wife, Joanne, were with me, and I said, "Now, Joanne, when I get to the part where I sing, 'this is not my wife you see,' then you come up there on the stage and I'm gonna hug you." Now Joanne was about 7 months pregnant with my granddaughter, Crystal and really showing. She came up rubbing her belly and gave me a big hug.

Them son-of-a-bitches went nuts, man! They gave me a standing ovation. It was un-damn-believable! First time I ever got a standing ovation. 'Bout the *only* time!

Brenda Byers recorded the first two songs for me and then Kevin Thomas did about 10, and I had Morning Star Studios in Naples do the last three that's on the tape—"Yankee Dollar," "Country Song Backwards" and "Somebody Stole My Boat."

The biggest mistake I ever made is that I took a little tape recorder to Faye in the hospital about six months or so before she died. And I said, "Honey, listen to this song that a guy and I put together." And I played "What Kind of Fish is That?"

When it was over, she looked at me and said, "Don't you know I'm dying, Stan?"

That'll melt your heart, baby. I never mentioned singing to her again. Never.

After that, it was just a few months later that she died, and that's when the Mullet Festival and all that comes into view. I started writing songs—they were coming to me again. Kevin and I made a song a month until he moved to Nashville. That threw me off kilter because he had a studio in his house and we could record our work.

When he came back after eight years in Nashville and saw what we were doing out here at Stan's with the shows, he couldn't believe it.

"Yankee Dollar"

If you ever wondered why I had that sign up there that says, "Stan's on Easter Sunday, a million dollars," well, this is for you.

The lyrics to the song go, *Let's give a cheer, cause the yankees are here / We're gonna make some money now!* We use that song for charities. I'll get up and sing it, and when people come up with a dollar, I'll shout out where they're from, and they'll give me the dollar.

But this is what got the "Yankee Dollar" song off the ground. One day at Stan's, I told the people, "Today I got a new song I want to sing called 'Yankee Dollar,'" and I said, "If I sing this song a million times and every time I sing it you give me a dollar, and if I sing it a million times, I'll have a million seller. Do you want me to have a million seller?"

And they all screamed, "Yeah!"

So I put a thermometer up there from zero to one million. We used to put the red marks as we collected. We got up only so far, and somebody finally said, "You're not doing so good with that Yankee Dollar are ya?"

I said "No, I'm not."

"Christmas Day"

"Christmas Day" is the only song Nashville gave me a contract on. But nobody's ever recorded it. The contract was with the Glazier Brothers Publishing Company in Nashville, 1966.

When the song plugger listened to it, he called in the boss, Chuck Glazier, and he said, "Yeah, give him a contract on the Christmas Song." I still have it today, but nobody's ever recorded it. If they do,

I'll still have the contract. I'd get a penny a record or three cents a sheet copy, the whole thing's laid out. They had just finished Glen Campbell's great hit, "Gentle On My Mind," and they gave me all the brochures on that, so they were legitimate. It's just that no one ever picked it up.

The great Bob Snyder, the sax player, recorded "Christmas Day" on a Christmas CD. I got several small royalty checks on that. In fact, they went from $30 or $40 down to six or seven cents as it kind of folded out. He did a beautiful job with a full band. Of course, he plays the lead on the clarinet. It's a great arrangement, but I just can't seem to get anybody to record it, although I have that feelin' in my heart that someday somebody will.

"Christmas Day" is all about Jesus' birthday. It has a religious touch to it, and it's a popular ballad type song. I sing it most every year at the lighting of the Christmas tree in Town Center on Marco because my buddy, Kevin Thomas, can play it.

Every song that I ever made up was made up by my voice, like if you take a guitar player and he writes a song with the guitar or a piano player writes with a piano. But I've always made them up with my voice. Kevin would know what chords I sang, and he would make the arrangements, so to speak. He would do the song, and I'd rehearse it with the tape, then I'd go to his studio and we would record the song. He would direct me, actually, in the recording of the song like the director in a big band would do.

I made about 10 songs with Kevin that way. The other three I made with Ray Nesbit and the Morningstar Band. They were "Yankee Dollar," "Stuck on a Sandbar" and "Country Song Backwards."

Then, a guy in Naples wrote me a song called, "Stan's in Goodland, Hung up again."

"Stan's In Goodland, Hung Up Again"

Now there's another story behind that one. After Faye's death, I was singing and performing a little bit in the bar. I performed with a guitar player from Ohio named John Stevens. We were getting some tourists in by that point.

Well, there was a street sign coming into Goodland that says, "GOODLAND," and it seems that every year somebody stole that sign and took it home as a souvenir. So one day, somebody came up to me and told me the sign was missing again.

Trying to be a good citizen, I called the county to tell them we need this road sign replaced. I got a gal on the phone—I don't think she was as dumb as me, but she was about my class.

I said, "I'm Stan in Goodland, and I want to tell you the Goodland road sign has been stolen, and we need the Goodland sign hung up again."

So about two weeks went by, and here come three Mexicans out there with a regular road sign that says, "Goodland Hung Up Again"!

Jim was a county road supervisor. He got in on this and loved to come to Stan's. Sometimes he'd get up on the stage and sing with me. He was a great fun-loving guy who could write songs. So when he heard this story, he wrote a song about it.

I thought, "Lord, I don't know how I can ever sing this song." So I got Wally Collins and Rex Roden, who were in a hot country band back in those days, and we went out in my boat one day in the Gulf off of Keewayden Island. They brought their guitars, and they taught me how to sing, "I'm in Stan's in Goodland Hung Up Again": *I got lots and lots of hang ups, some good, some real bad / I'm here at Stan's in Goodland, hung up again . . .*

Jim wrote the song, and it was a good one. Still today, people ask me to sing it. Jim moved out later on to Nashville. He passed away up there with cancer. His wife brought him back here and had me go on the boat with them and the family to do the ashes off the Marco bridge. That's what he wanted.

Over the last 21 years that we've been doing the show at Stan's on Sunday, I've rotated four bands for a variety effect. I've had Kevin Thomas and the Buzzard Band, Jeff Hilt & Don Riddle and the Stampede Band. I had Wally Collins and Rex Roden—good friends of mine—with the Hot Country Band. They played for me for about 20 years, but last year Wally moved to Savannah and Rex moved back to Ohio for one reason or another. So the Hot Country Band isn't with us now. In their place I have Norm and Debbie and the Hot Damn Band. To make the fourth, I took on another band a few months ago called Southern Cross. That's a married couple named Dean and Robin.

I went back to the studio a while back and did *The Other Side of Stan* with some of the old songs I learned to sing as a young man. I'd always wanted to do that. I used the arrangements of Perry Como, Frank Sinatra and Dean Martin. We sell quite a few CDs for not really being known. People call, and I ship them all over the country.

Nobody knew how the hell this was gonna turn out. I didn't even know myself. The Lord guided my path. Everywhere I went, He directed my path. I still believe it today. And I ask Him every day in the morning, "Please direct my path today."

≈ 16 ≈

CANCER

The big promise I made to Faye to get her to go along with me on this deal in Goodland was that I would build her another house. In the early '80s, I eventually acquired a lot in Goodland and built that house.

She loved it. She decorated and everything. I still live in that house today.

Well, in 1978 she developed colon cancer, but it was unknown to any of us. Her stomach hurt her, but she didn't admit how bad it was, that she was having some blood in her bowel movements. Since she didn't tell the doctors that, they diagnosed her with a nervous stomach. By the time it got around to where it was real bad, it was too late to save her.

We were doing well with the restaurant. I had a used Cadillac that had about 10,000 miles on it, and I was gonna pick my mother and step-dad up in Alabama, and we were going to take a month off and drive to California to see my oldest brother, Wally.

Well, we got as far as Tampa. We stayed all night there at Terra Verde, which the Mackle people owned. And Faye's stomach just erupted. Diverticulitis set in.

I thought she was going die right there before I could get her to the hospital, so we asked a big black fella to help us out, and he told us where the hospital was. We run her down there. They kept her all day and they said for me to give her juices. They let her out, but she did have a temperature. They suggested for me to bring her back down to Goodland.

She was so tough, she insisted that she was OK. So we spent the night in Terra Verde. A bunch of people were out there by the pool having this big lobster cookout and luau. It's gorgeous man!

So I said, "C'mon, Faye, let's go." She said, "I don't feel like goin' but you go." She was laying on a couch there.

So I brought her back some food, but she never ate—big lobster and all that. The next day, she took a bath to relieve her fever.

On our third morning at Terra Verde I woke up and thought to myself, "You're the dumbest son-of-a-gun I ever seen! There's somethin' *bad* goin' on here. She keeps telling you she's alright, and, dammit, she's tough, but somethin's *wrong!*"

So I packed her up in the car that day in the back seat and took her back to Marco. The doctor there put her in the hospital. The next morning, the X-ray showed she had colon cancer.

Then they operated. That was 1978. Between '78 and '83, she had eight major operations. They'd take part of the colon, 11, 12, 13 months later, we'd come back. Can't go to the restroom. They'd take another piece off. Then later, come back, take more. Then the next thing you know, they'd have to operate on her, take more out and put a bag on her. Then she gets over that and they take the bag off. That lasts about 10 months, then she has to come back and put the bag back on, permanently.

This went on eight times. I had to kiss her goodbye that many times.

On New Year's Day, 1983, she was home here with us and we were watching football. We were crazy football people, especially when Alabama was on.

She said, "I hate to ruin the game, but I think I gotta go to the hospital."

So Russ carried her out, she couldn't walk. She died 17 days later in the hospital.

But you know what? That was a blessing. That was a blessing. She'd suffered so much, and got so little. They had a bag on both kidneys and the bowels, so it was just awful, the pain. Oh, my God, it was awful. I prayed for her to die. "Please, Lord, let her die."

I know my wife's funeral in 1983 was the biggest funeral Marco's ever seen. We were already known all around, and she was very active in social clubs and the Goodland Civic Association. People used to come over a lot and just sit and talk with her because she just was that kind of person. She was a beautiful woman, and she had a lot of good sense. She kept *our* asses straight, I know that!

The flowers on her grave were piled up, just unbelievable. Josberger's Funeral Home had so many flowers in there, they were all around the wall, all around the casket, and all over the back.

We walked from the funeral home to the gravesite because it's that close. It was a helluva walk that day. A lot of people came, a lot of people.

My kids came over there with dark glasses on, I'll never forget it. I said, "Take them damn glasses off." I said, "You gonna look at her with your naked eyes, you understand? You ain't lookin' at her with no dark glasses on."

They never put them back on, either. It's a little thing, but it got to me. Forty-seven years old. They couldn't cure her. They operated on her eight major times in five years.

She was really something.

≈ 17 ≈

A LITTLE VOICE SAID,
"STAN . . . EVERY SUNDAY"

Just before Faye died, I had to sell the motel. We kept it for eight years. I had to let it go for what I paid for it because times were not yet booming there. I paid off some debt, and then we went strictly into the restaurant. I was also a fishing guide.

I was sort of getting back into music at that point, but all through those 12 years prior to it, I had no music in me. None whatsoever. I don't know what music was popular in the '70s, I was working so hard.

In the mid 80's I started writing songs again. It was based on inspirations from God and centered on the environment that I happened to be in at the time. That's when I came up with the "Buzzard Song," "What Kind of Fish is That?," "Yankee Dollar," and "Country Song Backwards."

My next door neighbor, A B. Martin, came over and asked me to do a mullet festival for the mullet fishermen. I said "No, I've got more than I can handle already just trying to keep my head above water. I don't need to be taking on anything else."

But he kept pursuing the idea, and I finally gave in. In 1985, we had the first Mullet Festival in a vacant lot across from Stan's owned by Mr. Curcie. We put it on the radio and surprisingly enough about 1,500 people showed up on a Sunday afternoon. It was a great day. We paid all the bills and had money left over.

The next year we decided to do it again and even more people showed up. We made more money. Then the next year, 1987, the Curcies said we couldn't use their vacant lot because somebody might get hurt.

We had had two successful events the previous two years, and it was just too bad we couldn't do it again. A little Italian lady that I knew very well had moved down from Jersey. She liked to come in the bar. One day, she said, "Stan, why don't you have the Mullet Festival here on your property."

I said, "Rose, dammit, I don't need no bullshit. We don't have room to have no festival over here."

She proceeded to tell me to take out the boat ramp, put this over here, put this in here and, there you go, plenty of room! I thought about it overnight. The next day I started doing just what she had said. I dragged the stage over and took out the boat ramp. My boys said, "Dad, what are you doing. Have you gone crazy?"

I said, "Yeah. I'm sick of all them fishermen. They don't do nothing but take up room with their trailers and they don't buy anything. We're going to do the Mullet Festival here."

We did the third Mullet Festival in 1987 on the stage at Stan's, again on Sunday afternoon. And honest to God my parking lot was full. The whole street was full. Goodland was *full* of people. I'm up there singing and doing the Buzzard Lope—I had written the song just for the Mullet Festival. It was designed so contestants would do the Buzzard Lope Dance, and the audience would select the best one as the Queen of the Festival, the Mullet Queen. Today, it's the Buzzard Lope Queen.

I got up Monday morning, paid every bill I could think of and, lo and behold, I had $1,600 left over.

A little voice quietly said, "Stan ... every Sunday. *Do this every Sunday.*" And that was the making of us.

We've done the Mullet Festival for 22 years now. It's been a big success. We've been on CNN with it one year, TBS another year, and local TV for about 18 years now. They haven't televised it for the last two or three years. We've gotten calls from all around the country from people having seen it on TV because sometimes they pick up local TV stuff and show it in different places. We've also been written up in a lot of papers for it.

Now I understand we're the 10th most popular outside thing to do in the state of Florida. A lady from Tallahassee was making a calendar, and we're going to be in it for the Mullet Festival.

I appreciate all the people who come to our place, especially for the Sunday show every week. We got friends all around the world on account of that Sunday show mostly. We've been doing it coming up on 23 years now. People call me from up north and write me letters and send different things. I even get some calls from England and Germany, and I'm just blessed to have a place where people come to.

It's a tourist place. I think that's most of the reason God sent me that song "Yankee Dollar." We use that song for charities, because most the time they'll give me money when I sing it. They'll just come up and hand me dollar bills.

All that is God-sent, the songs, the creating of the dance, the whole thing. It all just came to me from Him.

The parking lot struggle

In 1990, when we put the Sunday Show in, we were getting really nice crowds, especially in season. We had to have more parking then because we were getting overrun with crowds on Sunday.

So across the street is this big lot, which is right on the corner across the street from Stan's. I asked Joey Curcie, the guy who owned it, if I could park over there on Sunday, and he said it was okay.

Well, after a few months of that, the jealousy set in, and Joey said, "You know, I'm afraid somebody's gonna get hurt . . ."

I said, "Look, I need it so bad, how 'bout me payin' you a hundred dollars a Sunday?"

That'd be $400 a month. Joey was my next door neighbor. His dad was Ted Curcie, a rich man who developed all of this side of Goodland. He put in all the roads and the water and all that and had a big dirt pit out in the Everglades. He owns all the property on the left going out of Goodland over there on Hwy 92. He's got a bridge named after him called Curcie Bridge.

Unfortunately, his son couldn't handle being the son of a rich guy. He'd already been in trouble in Miami. He robbed a liquor store at gunpoint, and his dad got him out of prison a couple years later and put him over here in Goodland and let him live next door to *me*, which was a horrible mistake! The guy absolutely hated me, and hated anybody that crossed him.

So he was getting $100 a week from me for the parking. Well, a real estate lady came up to me one day and she said, "Stan, I got all this property for sale in Goodland that belongs to Ted Curcie," and she showed me the properties marked in yellow. And that parking lot was marked in yellow!

I said, "They're selling the parking lot? They never said nothin' to me!"

She said, "Well, I just don't think they want you to have it."

I said, "Well, they don't. Okay. Can I make a bid that they don't know about?"

She said, "Well, you can get somebody to buy it for you."

So I decided to call Glen Tucker, an attorney on Marco and a good friend. I asked him if he'd do that for me. They wanted $150,000 for it. He agreed to help me out.

I offered them a hundred and something thousand, and we settled on $125,000. I went into debt for it. But they didn't know it was me.

Well, Joey and I got into a little argument one time down there about the dog. He had a dog that was bad, and I ran him off one day. Joey was a maniac in his head, he really was.

So July came along—this was the early '80s because Faye was still alive and we were worried about him coming and doing something to our house or whatever he might do. So this all went on with him till after she passed away.

So the sale goes through, but we can't tell Joey. When the summer comes, I told everyone, "Don't park in the lot across the street, because we don't need to and the guy charges me $100 if somebody parks over there." Even though I got the lot, I just was hiding it.

Joey didn't know at this point that I had bought the property. So he called me and he said, "Where's my hundred dollars?"

I said, "Well, Joey, I hate to tell you this, but I heard somebody bought the property."

"Oh, no. No, no, no. Didn't nobody buy that property. I still own it," he said.

I said, "Well, really, I hate to lower this on you, son, but I bought the damn property and I've been payin' on it for the last three months."

He said, "Oh you did?"

I said, "Yeah, I did."

He said, "Well, I guess that means I won't have to cut the grass no more."

I said, "No, you won't."

So he hung up.

The next Sunday, while I'm down there singing and doing the show, Joey took my water hose from my front foyer out there, knocked a hole in the side of my door, turned the water hose on and flooded my living room. It was one of those sunken living room—now a *truly* sunken living room. I thank God it didn't get the rest of the house. He did that all afternoon. When I came home, I had water a foot deep in my living room.

So we called the law, and he wouldn't come out of the house, and we knew he'd done it. He wouldn't show his face or answer the door. We couldn't prove it. My son, Russ, wanted to kill him. Believe it or not, there was a man in Naples I knew who loved my place because I'd helped him out when he needed help. He heard about this, and *he* wanted to go kill him. I wouldn't let him.

So we went on and lived by Joey and every now and then my window on the bedroom side would be knocked out or a dead black cat would show up in my truck, or I'd send somebody over here to cut my grass and he'd run 'em off saying, "Don't get on my property with that lawn mower!"

He was just a maniac. Everybody in Goodland hated him. He duct-taped one dog's mouth shut. Poor dog almost died before they could get it off. Joey bit some woman's face, ruined some guy's condo with his own fire extinguisher when he was up north.

A couple of young kids hit him in the head with a pipe one day, liked to kill him, but they didn't hit him hard enough. He was on drugs and selling drugs. The cops never would do nothing with him. The Curcie's had too much money. His dad was too influential. Every time he'd get in trouble, his dad would pay him out of it.

But of all things, believe it or not, I prayed for him. I really did. I knew it was the thing to do. He didn't know what he was doing. He was in darkness.

I would always speak to Joey, but I didn't want to have much to do with him. I was always leery of him, but I'd speak to him when I was in the yard. His dad passed away, so he was really notorious now because he's got the whole run of Goodland. He's got all of this property and all of this money. He was just the cock of the walk. But I would always speak to him, then get away from him and get back in the house just as soon as I could.

He was sick. He'd already been getting sick with all of the drugs he'd done. He was having liver and stomach problems too, I think. He got married and ended up having three kids. I thought he was going to come around, but he still had that behind him.

I was out there in the yard one day, in about 2003, and he said, "Y'know Stan, I just wanna tell you something. I'm the guy that flooded your house."

I said, "I know that."

He said, "Now do I owe you any money?"

I said, "No. Just telling me is good enough for me."

He said, "I'm really sorry about that."

So I figured from that, he must be thinking that he was having real trouble. But he lagged on and went to the hospital a couple of times for different things. He'd always get out. But everybody in Goodland— it's hard sayin'—they were wishing he'd die.

But he paid everybody to do things for him. The only ones who liked him were the ones he paid money to, to do things around his house.

One morning I woke up, and someone told me Joey died that night. My neighbor had died.

They explained that he fell in the shower, through the glass door, and cut his stomach open and was bleeding to death. He drove himself to the Urgent Care Center and died over there.

I ran into his wife one day at Publix. She came up to me and said, "Stan, I'm Kathy Curcie, and I want to thank you for being so nice to Joey while he was alive."

≈ 18 ≈

GOOD THING I AIN'T
TRYING TO HIDE

Of all things, recently, my girl friend, Lynn Espejo, saw this table on TV that you can strap yourself in and it turns you upside down for blood flow, circulation and back trouble.

So I said, "Well, I'll call the 800 number and order it, then I'll always have it, and any of us can use it."

So I get a gal on the line, and I said, "I want to order that table."

So she asks for my phone number, then says, "You're in Goodland, Florida?"

I said, "Yes. Damn, you know more about me than I do!"

She said, "Is your name Stan?"

I said it was.

She said, "Are you Stan of 'Stan's'?"

I said, "Ya."

She said, "I know you."

I said, "You do?"

She said, "Ya, I've done the Buzzard Lope at your place!"

I said, "Where you at?"

She said, "Virginia."

I laughed like crazy about that!

I walked into a bar up in Ohio called the Golden Ram, which was a stage coach stop in the old days. We went down to the bar and a gal started doing the Buzzard Lope. She just looked right at me and started.

She said, "I know you, you're Stan!"

I said, "Son-of-a-gun, I didn't know I was known up *here*!"

I guess it's a good thing I'm not trying to hide.

≈ 19 ≈

FROM MULLET TO BUZZARD

When A.B. Martin and I were planning the first Mullet Festival, I figured if we're gonna sit around here drinking and waiting on these mullet fishermen, oh, man, we gotta have something better than that. So all of a sudden, this song starts coming to me about the buzzards. And, as the Lord is my witness, I started singing the "Buzzard Song."

So I said, "A.B., I got an idea. While the contestants are out fishing, let's get these gals in a dance contest, get 'em to do this Buzzard Song—it talks about dancin' . . . We'll let the audience select a Mullet *Queen*." He agreed and we got some publicity out on it.

For that first dance, I didn't have a stage. We just did it in the back of Stan's. So we go over there and have the fishermen come in, they weigh the fish, then the party goes on across the street where the homemade stage is in 1985 on the empty lot. We used that lot for two years, then moved over to the stage at Stan's in '87.

Now, as we're rocking along, somewhere around 1990, the county passed a law that you can't mullet fish on the weekends. That ended that, but the timing was perfect because the Mullet Festival, well, it just wasn't goin' as good as we'd hoped. It got a little *too* competitive instead of fun. So when the county decided that, well, I thought, "Great!

We can keep up the party without the competition." So we went from the Mullet King and Queen to the Buzzard Lope Queen.

Now Anna Yamonis and I were going together then, and she was a part of the Buzzard Lope's creation. She's the one who came up with some great ideas and made our costumes.

She was a great promoter of what we were doing. Every time I went to Marco to sing, she'd be promoting us over there. She put the boutique in and started selling all the paraphernalia with "Stan's" on it—the hats, shirts and the buzzard thing. She came up with the buzzard logo which we use today. It's just made a success out of what we do. I truly love her for it and always will, for what she did for us. She's a great gal. Today she's married to a wonderful guy, John Carter. With the help of John's daughter, Fia, and Fia's husband, Steve, they run the Island Woman Boutique. They're great people.

In 1990, Queen Mary Martin got into the Buzzard Contest, which we have every year on the third weekend of January, and she won it. Mary lives in Naples. Most of the queens are from up north. Well, Mary loves to dance. She's a crowd pleaser—they just love her, and it adds to the show.

1995 was the 10th year of the Mullet Festival. We have a new Buzzard Queen every year. Although a lot of my queens will come and help the others out on Sunday, they'll wear their costume and dance, but they're not in the contest.

Well, we decided if we could get all the queens we could find for the first 10 years, when we get that 10th year queen, we'd let all of *them* compete for the Queen of the Decade.

We got seven of them—from New York, Michigan, Ohio, all the way down to Goodland, Isles of Capri. I want you to know that Mary Martin won the Queen of the Decade hands down! They went crazy over her.

When we got to 20 years at Stan's, which is a score, we did the same thing, and Mary was competing against 14 other queens that we found. She won that one too!

So Mary Martin is three queens including Queen Mary of the Decade and the Score.

We used to have a little stuffed animal dog that walked. But when we laid him on his side and turned him on, his legs would kick like he was dying. And we had a little stuffed buzzard that was sitting right over the top of him looking at him. The kids would love the hell out of it. We'd put it right on the dance floor while we did the Buzzard Song.

One little girl from Indiana—she was so precious, she was only about four. She picked that little black buzzard up, it was only about 10″ tall, and she picked that little buzzard up and she hugged it like it was the most precious little thing in this world.

And, bein' a weak heart, I had to give it to her.

≈ 20 ≈

WHERE WERE YOU WHEN ANDREW BLEW THROUGH?

If I was going to do something special every Sunday at Stan's, I knew I had to get a band here. Jay Robert, an entertainer on Marco was playing in the area, and I was telling him about it.

He knew a good bluegrass-country band out of Tampa that would come down. So they came, and I advertised them and we did the show. Well, that's when I woke up Monday morning with $1,600 left in my pocket despite paying every possible bill—finally not trying to figure who to pay and who to put off!

Some guys get wind of our show's success over on Marco, and the next you know, I got the Back Porch Band which became the Stampede Band with Jeff Hilt. I figured we better rotate bands and have a variety show, so people would say, "Look, let's go over there because you never know what's happening over there!" We had to do the buzzard dance every Sunday, and I figured we could create a little activity around that.

(The bands we rotate today, January 2006, are the Stampede Band with Jeff Hilt and Don Riddle, the Buzzard Band with Kevin Thomas, the Hot Damn Band with Norm and Deb, and the Southern Cross Band with Dean and Robin.)

It just gets better and better, and all of a sudden it's the place to go on Sunday. Fortunately, I acquired the lot across the street from me—almost an acre. I went in debt for that lot, but it saved us because it gave us some big parking. That was another God-send to me. So ever since then, we've been hitting at 'em real strong, working hard.

Well, the 1992 hurricane comes along. "Where were you when Andrew came through?"

We owed about $23,000 on the restaurant, and of all times, it was the second time in my life that I had insurance on the place—fire, wind, peril and flood. It tore us up about $110,000.

Andrew knocked the roof off. Water got through and wet all the floors and everything else inside. We had a $10,000 deductible. I called my kids in and I said, "Listen guys, now we gonna have to put this place back together." Thank God it was in the summer when we were only open on the weekends. There's no business here off-season.

We put a new floor in the restaurant, had a new roof put on, got new facilities, got some new stuff in the kitchen, and we worked hard. We ate up the $10,000. We got all the bids we could get, then we would do the work. The insurance people loved that. They worked with me on that, and they was tickled to death that we would do our own work.

So after the insurance payout, I had enough money to pay the place off. I couldn't believe it. It was God's will. The hurricane skirmished us enough to do just a little bit of damage—not enough to close us down—and we were going to pay the restaurant off. What a happy cat I was! We were in debt from January 1970 to August 1992—twenty-two years.

≈ 21 ≈

HE DIRECTS MY PATH

Every once in a while when I'd be working real hard, I'd just *stop* and say, "Thank you, Jesus, for giving me the strength and energy to do this. Because I know there are people layin' in hospitals all over America that wish they could do this. And I am. Thank you."

I don't go to church, but I am a man of faith. I consider Jesus to be my partner in this life.

That's really what makes me tick, believing in God. I like the verse in Proverbs 3:5–6 that says, "Trust in the Lord with all your heart, and lean not on your own understanding. In all your ways acknowledge Him, and He shall direct your paths."

I totally believe that once you're in His hands, He directs your path.

Faye and I were baptized in the mid-'60s at a Baptist church in Hialeah, Florida. That's where I confessed Christ again. That was the second time. The first time was in Alabama. The Bible says you need to confess Christ in front of your fellow man and be baptized in the Holy Spirit.

So that's the way I live, and God knows I'm a sinner like everybody else, but I do believe. So I want to tell you a little story right quick about that.

One of my good customers was Chuck Smalley from Iowa. He was a self-made millionaire who started off laying blocks and wound up with three cement companies. He gave freely of himself with no motive. He didn't go to church either, but, like me, he was a spiritual fellow. Before he died, one of his requests was that I preach his funeral and that we have it at Stan's.

This man died, and it was time to have the funeral at Stan's. The night before it, I prayed because Lord knows I'm not a preacher and had certainly never preached a funeral.

We had the ceremony there on the stage. I was so sad and I had the people so sad. I was stuttering, looking bad, didn't know what to say.

All of a sudden I saw his face smiling at me just as clear as could be. And he spoke to me. He said, "Stan, you're too sad. Don't be sad."

I said, "Folks, excuse me a minute. I see Chuck's face." And I got all choked up. But I kept going. "He's smiling at me and he says we're too sad. He says it's alright to cry but it's also alright to laugh. He says he had a great life. He was a great man and we're going to miss him."

Then I said, "Would anybody like to say something about Chuck?" Three people got up and spoke about their remembrances of Chuck. Later people told me I did a great job, it was a wonderful funeral. But I didn't do anything. I just listened to Chuck.

About 15 years ago a lady came in the bar from Philadelphia. I didn't know her. She didn't know me. But another lady I did know said she was a fortune teller. That she could read me.

"Oh hell no. I don't want nobody to tell me nothing about me."

Later after a few drinks there was nobody else there at the bar except these two ladies and my bar maid. The Philadelphia lady walks over to me, takes my hand and says, "You're going to make a lot of money entertaining."

She moved her hand to my chest and said, "If this doesn't stop you." That got my attention because I've always suffered from bronchial asthma. I don't smoke and never could smoke. The next day I went and got a chest X-ray which was OK.

The next thing she said was, "I see fire in the deep, on a big boat."

Sure enough three weeks later I was out fishing and my boat caught on fire.

She said I had a brother in California which I do and a daughter whose name starts with B. That would be Becky. She said, "Your wife has passed away and you've never found anybody to replace her." True.

She said, "You've got no money. It's coming in one hand and going out the other." Shortly after that I found out someone was stealing my money.

Even though she was right about so many points I didn't put much stock in it until just recently. Because she said, "I see a problem with your legs." I figured that was probably my older brother out in California. But today he's walking fine and I'm hobbling around with two knee replacements.

She did tell me one other thing. I know a lot of people don't have much faith. But I do and always have. She said, "Stan, you've got a guardian angel on your shoulder and it's there all the time. He or she is watching over you and is there all the time." That's what she said.

Lord have mercy, I believe that.

And when I die I'm going to have my funeral on the Sunday stage at Stan's. The band knows to play two songs. First, "When the Saints Go Marching In." And then "The Buzzard Lope." I've already got it arranged with my sons and the bands, and I've already asked a Baptist preacher to preach my eulogy when I go.

My gravesite is ready right next to Faye's. The dates on Faye's tombstone read "3/7/1935 – 1/17/1983 My tombstone reads "Stan Gober, 4/30/1926 – ."

After I'm laid to rest in the Marco Cemetery everybody will come back to Stan's for the party. Russell will foot the bill for the party. He's big enough too, to be sure nobody gets carried away being overly sad.

After all, when anybody has had as great a life as I've had, it calls for a celebration, not sadness.

≈ 22 ≈

DRUGS INVADE GOODLAND

Some time during the mid-'70s, Goodland and the Everglades and the Ten Thousand Islands became a major stomping ground for drug smugglers. They started bringing in all this stuff from South America or wherever. They dropped it in the Gulf of Mexico from airplanes and boats went out and picked it up.

It was so wide open that they turned Goodland into a damn hell-hole for drugs. I prided myself on being a drug-free place in Goodland back in those days. And I kept my kids off of it. I preached to them, I coached them like a football coach. I told them, "You're gonna go to prison, you gonna lose your life and if you go to jail for that crap, don't call me!"

Everyone around there knew what was happening, but a lot of them just turned their heads. Me, I'm outspoken about it.

We used to close the restaurant on Mondays back then so we could get provisions in Naples. One Monday, some druggie shot through the front of my building with a .357 magnum three times! The bullets went through the window into the back wall. I called the police, and they dug the pellets out. And they never said another word about it.

Anytime Faye and I called them about something we heard was going down that night, we'd never hear anything else about it from the police. We didn't seem to have any help from the police at all. Les Binns, our deputy sheriff for Marco, had already left by then, retired or whatever. He wasn't in the game.

Finally we bought the little house across the street from the restaurant and moved over there. That parking lot now that we have between Stan's and that little house on the corner was just high weeds. It didn't belong to me. There just wasn't anybody taking care of it. And sometimes we would get caught in there, between smugglers bringing stuff in and out of Goodland. The cops would park their car way down the road and get packages out of my phone booth in front of the building, then go get back in the car and leave. Now that was suspicious.

My son, Russ, was a teenager. He said, "Dad, you better stop talkin' about 'em, they gonna kill you!"

It was some bad days.

Ted Morgan, my neighbor, was a fishing guide, and he got into smuggling. He told me one day, "Stan, I see you're adding onto your building."

I said, "Ya, I'm tryin' to get a liquor license."

He said, "You need the money? I got plenty of money."

But I *knew* where it was coming from, so I said, "No man, I don't need any money."

So he kept on smuggling until one night somebody called him—it had to be somebody he knew—and asked him to come up Hwy 92, and that's where they found him, in the canal with three bullet holes in his head. He had a Rolex watch on, thousands of dollars in his pocket. They didn't take nothin' but his life. He got mixed up with it. I don't know how. That's the kind of things that were happening here.

We had a guy down at the Barge motel who blew his head off with a shotgun with rock music going as loud as it'd go.

We had some people put a cross on that first turn going toward Marco, where those gray buildings are, every year for a kid named Paul. The people who did drugs with him put it there. He was walking down the dark road in the middle of the night when somebody ran him over and killed him.

We had a gal in a houseboat down around here somewhere, and she committed suicide.

You could get drugs. The bell runners and the boys over there at the Marco Marriot knew exactly where you could get anything you wanted. That's how bad it was.

One day a dressed-up guy from the Collier County court came down to me and said, "Stan, here's the latest picture, do you know her?"

I said, "Well, I've seen her, but she don't come in here much."

He said part of her sentence is that she can't drink in a public place. She drank up at the Barge and at the Little Bar, but she never came around us.

I said, "Sir, do you think you could give us some help down here?"

He said, "From what?"

I said, "Drugs. It's all over the place. 360 degrees from my place there are smugglers all over."

He said, "Well, ya. I, uh, ya, I can mention it."

I said, "Well, I wish you would tell somebody, some agent that would come down here and help us out, 'cause it's all over."

He said, "Okay."

The next day, Russ got his beginner's driver's license. He was almost 17, and he was somewhere on Marco when the cops stopped him, jerked him out of his car, and said, "Boy, if you do anything wrong, we're gonna put you in the jail. You understand that?"

Russ told me, "Dad, I didn't do nothin' wrong. I don't know *why* they did that to me."

I said, "I think I know."

That to me was proof that I'd stepped on somebody's toes again.

A guy came down one day. He was a big burly guy. Every son of a bitch here was running drugs 360 degrees from my place. They were ruining our country and our kids. This guy named every damn one of them by name! I couldn't believe it. I'd never seen the guy in my life. Now Reagan hadn't been elected long, and in 1981 he declared war on the smugglers.

So the guy told me, "We gonna get them all. We have the authority to get them all."

I said, "But sir, I don't think you understand. The cops are crooked from Fort Myers down. They're all in cahoots."

He said, "Stan, we got the authority to get them too. We're comin' straight from the government."

And, damn, they had a shootout down there at that Old Fish House and put all them guys in jail. They surrounded Everglades City after a few months and put them all in jail.

This guy said to me, "If you ever see me again, I'll be in a mullet skiff with a woman." I never saw him again. He had gone undercover.

But I was friendly with all of these people who were into drugs and smuggling when they'd come to my place. I'd tell them, "You guys are screwin' your life up. You gonna go to prison or you gonna lose your life."

So many of them came back to see me after they got out of prison. One guy carved a big buzzard out of wood while he was in prison. Another one brought a banjo to me, because he knew I was into music.

My good buddy, Albert West was a notorious smuggler. He worked over at Marco in construction. He ran the Barge. He was a great boatsman. He was 6´2˝—a guy who never took his eyes off your eyes when he talked to you. He had nerves of steel, a real John Wayne type.

He had spent a lot of time in prison because he was the kingpin down here at the Old Fish House. But he and I got to be friends.

When the smuggling started, I got an inkling that he was involved in it because a little guy named Chuck, who washed dishes, told me he was. So I confronted Albert and told him, "I'm gonna have to get you out of here, Albert, 'cause I can't stand that stuff. I don't want my family around this kind of stuff. I'm sorry, man. We've been friends awhile, but you're gonna have to take your boat and find another place to dock it."

So he went down to the Old Fish House, and he got in with them cats. They had a big walk-in cooler that they stowed marijuana in.

When the shoot-out happened, man, he was shooting at the helicopter—from the ground to the helicopter—but he got away.

He built a big house in Golden Gate with a big high fence and big bright lights. His wife was an animal person, so they had horses down there and everything, even some big spotted cats that were bigger than house cats. He was really a kingpin.

When the Feds got all their charges together, they sent two guys over to Albert's house. They said they were from the Humane Society and they needed to check out their animals. That's how they got in. When they got in, they flipped it around and said, "We come to get you!"

The story was that she let the cats out of the room they were in, and these guys were ready for them. They put him in prison. He stayed there a long time. When he got out, one of the first places he came was Stan's.

I asked him, "Was it bad on ya?"

He said, "Naw, I had one there try to give me some trouble, but I got his ass straightened out, then I never had no problems."

He was thinking about going down to Mexico to start a catfish farm. He came back a couple times, and then I don't know where he went. I don't know what happened to him.

After Reagan got in, that's when the ax fell on the smugglers, around '85 or '86. Reagan declared war on them. All of a sudden the rage hit Goodland and Everglades City and all around the coastal areas. The government came out with a big cigarette boat called *Blue Thunder*. It had such powerful engines in it because the smugglers could outrun the regular local marine patrols. They put three or four big engines on there. They docked *Blue Thunder* on Marco at the old yacht club. If the wind was blowing right, you could hear them start that thing up all the way over here in Goodland. You could hear it coming up the river.

They had AWACs planes flying around too. They covered the coast, and they'd see everything that moved. If necessary, they'd send *Blue Thunder* out there to get 'em. It was full of DEA guys, trained men, and they'd start nullifying the coast. Then when they nullified the coast, that's when they pulled the string and got it all done. That was a good thing.

Today, if there's anything going on here, it's just social stuff. I don't know of any smuggling going on here now. I've told the police on Marco that I'd really appreciate it if they'd put an officer over at my place on Sunday because I really don't want that stuff around.

I get on that stage today and I tell the kids, "I don't give a damn how long your hair is or who your friends are and all that stuff. Just don't do no drugs, it'll ruin your life. You won't even know what's happenin' to you." I say, "You parents tell these little kids! Don't let 'em get on that stuff. It'll kill 'em."

We lived through the smuggling days, and we played the game straight, which is part of why we're still here. I know they checked us out, though. I don't know how many agents came in there trying to see where we stood. I've always been outspoken *about* where I stood. They never saw anything in the place that would make them think we were any other way.

When Faye passed on, we were making ends meet. We were able to go on a vacation before she died and build a house. We had enough business to make it work. We didn't need no smuggling—wouldn't never do that to make money anyway.

≈ 23 ≈

PULL THE ANCHOR
AND MOVE A LOT

Herb Robinson, the guy who sold me Stan's, advised me to get my fishing guide license, which I did in Miami. I told Herb I didn't know anything about taking people fishing. He said, "Nothing to it. Just pull the anchor and move a lot."

You know what was funny about me being a fishing guide? The Goodland locals didn't accept me at first. They said I brought Miami money over here and I was an outsider, and they wouldn't have nothin' to do with me.

In fact, they talked about me real bad. They said I didn't have any guide license and I didn't know what I was doing. They said all I could do was get stuck on a sandbar, and all I could catch was catfish.

That got me because though I don't mind anybody talking about me, I just would rather them at least try to tell the truth. So I made 50 copies of my guide license, and I put them all over the posts on Marco and everywhere, showing that I was a certified guide. I thought if they're gonna talk about me, I want them to know the truth!

Captain Catfish

When they were talking about me so hard like that, I was so stubborn. I wouldn't try to find out how the other captains were fishing. I could have seen their boats and thought, "Oh, they're fishin' over there. I'll go over there tomorrow." I just wouldn't do that. I had a CB, and they were all on CBs. I could have gotten my CB and listened in because they were all buddies. I was just too stubborn to say, "I need you." I'd think, "I gotta partner (Jesus), I don't need *you*! I'm gonna treat you right. I ain't gonna treat you like you're treatin' me."

So I went to the *Eagle* newspaper, and I put an ad in. Since they said I couldn't catch nothin' but catfish, I put an ad in the *Eagle* that said, "Come to Goodland and fish with Captain Catfish!"

So now I've grown a beard, and I got an old straw cowboy hat with a string on it, so it won't blow off, and I looked the part. I wore cutoffs, man, I really looked like a local.

They would come in that door after reading that ad, and they'd say to my wife out front, "Is Captain Catfish around here?" And she'd say, "Ya, he's in the back!"

I used to get letters to Captain Catfish for years after we gave it up. So I capitalized on what they were doing to me.

I got fishing trips, and we started making it good, and Faye stopped cryin' and raisin' hell around there. Then we got respect from the neighborhood, and eventually some of the guys came around.

But those fishermen, they never really came around to give me the time of day until somewhere in the late '70s when I put in a boat rail. A couple fellers helped me put it in so I could pull boats out of the water right next to the little house by the restaurant. It was a railroad system. And Lexie, the carpenter, made me a big body for the rail with railroad wheels on it, and angles and everything to put a boat on. It had a winch, so we could lower this thing down in the water on the railroad track and pull the boat up on it. We had the electric winch, and we pulled the boat out of the water and blocked it up, and we could work on our boats.

Now, these local fishermen saw this. Then they came over with their tails between their legs. See, up to this point, they all had trouble changing their props, and they had trouble cleaning their boats. They'd go to a mud flat out there on high tide and set their boats on it. When the tide went out, it'd be dry, so they'd stay on the boat and get out in the mud and push the boat over, prop it up with some boards and do one side, in the mud. Then push it over to the other side of the boat, do that side, and wait for the tide to come in. Then they'd float it off.

Now when they saw *this* . . . here they come!

"I was wonderin' . . . what would you charge me if I was to pull my boat up to change my prop?"

Now we're talking about all 25 to 30-foot boats, no bigger.

So I said, "How 'bout $20?"

"You'd do that for me?"

I said, "Ya!"

Then they come around later, "How much would you charge if we could paint our boat here?"

I said, "I'll tell you what I'll do. I'll charge you a dollar per foot, and I'll give you three days!"

They said, "Oh, my God! You will?"

Now, they're talkin' to me! I was being led by God, my partner, and I was out-foxin' them everywhere I went and being nice to them at the same time, which is the way you *should* do. The Bible says if you're nice to your enemies, it's like pouring hot coals on their heads. I was really enjoying it. I loved them asking me to help them because I loved doing it.

I do believe in my heart that there's still some of 'em that still hate me for moving here and changing "my part" of Goodland. If you'd have seen it before, it was just living and whatever the hell happened.

After I got here, and started meeting a lot of people from up north through the restaurant, and they started liking it and started buying stuff, things changed. And down in this side of Goodland, people started buying these little run down, beat up trailers and putting nice little cabins in and redoing places. Lexie was one of the first ones to do it. He bought a little trailer down there and put a cathedral roof over it and it looked like a little beautiful mansion.

Goodland started changing when people trimmed the hedges and cut the grass and just generally taking care of business. *That's* when Goodland started changing.

People are fussin' like crazy about Goodland changing *now*. They should have been here *then!* That makes me laugh. They're worried about Goodland changing, they should have seen it before!

You could lay down in the field across the street and nobody'd even see you.

Saved By a Beer Can

I was a fishing guide for 16 solid years, and the last six or eight I deep-sea fished. When you deep-sea fish, any time you go offshore, there's a chance that anything can happen. So I was always very cautious of the Gulf, and I paid attention.

One day, my buddy Warren Stewart came to me and he said, "Stan, I got some friends out fishin' and they haven't been back. A guy came in on a CB and said they was in trouble." (See, back in those days the CBs were all we had. This is going back 25 or 30 years.)

I said, "Well, hell, I'll go out there, do you know which way they are?"

He said, "Ya, they're such-and-such degrees off of Cape Romano."

So he and I went out. Now my boat was a 28-foot twin engine inboard cruiser. Well, when you're running along and you're on a plane, of course you're up in the air. The bow is up, but the stern is back. Most all of those kind of boats have a stern pump, in case you get to taking in water when you're on a plane like that and don't realize it. Unbeknownst to me, my pump is out, and I was taking on water the whole time I was going out there for 25 miles!

When we found the lost party right before dark, I pulled back on the throttle and we leveled off to swing around, throw them a line and start pulling them in because they had engine trouble. About that time, my pump goes off—my other pump in the middle of the boat was pumping more than it usually does.

I said to Warren, "Warren, I don't know, but this pump's still runnin'. Might be somethin' wrong." I was on the bridge, so I said, "Pull the hatch-cover down there over that engine, will ya?"

He pulled it, and, man, my boat was about a foot full of water! It was up to the cupping on the shaft. I jumped off of there. We started throwing water out of that boat with buckets and got the young man off the other boat. He was about 16 years old. We got four hatch-covers off and were throwing water every which way.

We got it down to where we could see where the water was coming in. The sea-cocks are in the deck of the boat, under the deck, and they bring in the sea water that goes through a filter, and around the engines. Well, a sea-cock had worked loose, because it was screwed down at the base, and it had worked loose so the water was coming into the boat *and* into the circulation pump. It was kind of offset under one of the covers.

We took a beer can and squashed it and pushed it down in there and drove it between the deck and the top of the sea-cock to put pressure on it to keep it down. To take all this out is a job. You really need to do this out of water, because when you take that sea-cock loose, it's over the hole where the water's gonna come in. So we jammed it with a beer can and pumped the boat out.

Needless to say, we didn't go fast, we came on in kinda slow. By the time we got to Goodland, like 3 a.m., my whole family was worried to death because we had no radio contact. The CBs were only good for five or six miles. I finally radioed them when I got to the Goodland Marina, and told them we were in. They were all drunk.

A Close One: Outswimming the Boat

After fishing offshore five or six years, I got very leery of fishing offshore by myself, so any time I was going, I'd tell the guys around the bar, "Listen, I'm goin' deep sea fishin' tomorrow. I got a charter if any of you guys wanna follow me out there."

Well, in this particular case, there were some guys from out of town and they wanted to go. They had two boats, and one of the guys was a sports writer for the *Tampa Tribune*. So we go out at Caxambas Pass. They're following me, and this time I have a 26′ inboard boat with one engine.

It was one of those absolutely beautiful Marco days—blue sky, calm water, the sun's shining, it's just gorgeous. It just makes you so happy to be alive.

We got offshore about two and a half or three miles, and my motor quit. Well, we pulled the cover, and we were all looking at it. I got four guys chartered from a convention at the Marriott hotel. I don't know a damn thing about motors, I just don't. I'm not mechanically inclined, and I just don't care about it. One guy thought he was, and he started checking around and said, "I think you got a bad coil."

Well, I knew where there was an old Ford truck in Goodland, by the wayside, so I said, "I know where this old Ford truck with a motor is, if one of you guys will take me in, we got plenty of time and a good start, we can get the coil."

So we did. We put it on. It didn't work. The only thing I knew then was to just have one of them pull me back, so they did.

So it's this beautiful calm day, and we're all coming back, but they got a long line out to me from their wooden boat, and it's tied on a 4 x 4 wooden stack that goes up and goes down to a 2 x 2 with a cross on it with a red and green light on the cross.

It was such a long line that I would fishtail this way, then the boat would jerk me that way, and I was just being jerked around right and left.

I said, "Hold it a minute, let's take a little slack out of the line and see if I can get a little closer to ya."

Now one of my passengers, a customer said, "I'll get it!" All we had was a windshield to step over to get this.

I said, "No, no, I got it."

And I stepped up over and put my arm around this 4 x 4 post to get the line off. Now when I did the boat snapped around, jerking me, and the whole thing came off. Since I had my arm around it, it jerked me off the boat and into the water.

I went into the water so fast with the momentum of the boat, that I guess I panicked because I didn't open my eyes. I'm a good swimmer, so I started swimming underwater. I came up, and the boat hit me in the head.

I went back under, swam a little faster, came up and the boat hit me in the head again. Well, I should have realized it, but I must have been a little bit panicked, because I didn't realize I was swimming along with the boat.

Now, I figured this was my last chance. I had to get out from under this boat. I still didn't open my eyes, but I swam *really* fast and hard. I mean I was swimming as fast as I possibly could. When I came up, I was about a foot behind the boat. *Behind the boat!*

Well, when I did, the guys on the boat didn't know what the hell had happened to me. So they're standing there with one of those little life preserver cushions, looking for me. Well, when I popped up out of the water, one of them threw me a cushion. And when he did, honest to God, I climbed right up on top of it like a bullfrog! I'm breathin' hard and I'm scared to death.

Then they threw a line over to me and pulled me in. They were pulling me into the boat saying, "Captain, are you alright?"

I said, "No, man, I need a drink—*bad*. I almost lost my life."

The sports writer from the *Tribune* sent me a copy of the sports section with a headline in big letters: "These Fishermen Had Nothing But Bad Luck," and he told the whole story in the paper.

I tell you what, man, I stayed in all afternoon after that. That one really affected me. That was close. I was going down for the third time. *That was close.*

≈ 24 ≈

BRUSHES WITH HOLLYWOOD

Some film people came down in 1992 to make a family movie called *Captiva Island*. It's about a young kid whose dad wants him to follow him in a big, successful rich man's business in New York. But this kid is about 12 or 14, and he wants to fly instead.

So he comes down to Captiva Island in Florida to visit some friends, and it turns out, he won't go back. So his dad comes down looking for him and they get involved with a guy on Captiva Island—which is actually Goodland—that has a big wooden boat. He's a treasure hunter. He's a drinker, but he knows there's treasure out there, he knows a boat sunk out in the Gulf. He's planning to find it.

Ernest Borgnine is in the movie and Arte Johnson and Banana George. Banana George is over 80 years old, and he waterskis barefoot. He plays himself in the movie.

Well, they got *me* to play the bartender in *my own bar*. So I had two lines, and one was right on the camera. When Banana George walked up, I was supposed to say, "How ya doin', George? I haven't seen you in a long time," which I did—three times. And we had an audience of 20 or 30 people, and they clapped every time I got through my line. They ended up cutting that line, but that was only for that scene.

The other scene I was in was when the treasure hunter was drinking beer at the bar and doing something called "depth charges." That's when you drop a shot in a shot glass into your glass of beer. His name was B.J., and he was a good guy from Texas. He and I really had a good friendship.

So, the only part you see of me in the movie is my back when I'm drawing a beer right there at that little bar, and I walk off, and when I do, B.J. hollers, "Stan, hit me with another one of them depth charges!" And I say, "Comin' right up B.J!"

I made $516 for that! I actually had to get signed up for the Actor's Guild for the movie or I couldn't have gotten paid.

I was in one other scene when I was just cleaning up the parking lot. What was funny, I was B.J.'s dad before the end of the movie came around, so they had to make me look older than I was. I had to go to Makeup in a big trailer down by the Calusa. It was a professionally done movie.

Now, I let all the cast eat at Stan's every day for lunch that was catered by an Indiana guy who they'd brought with them. And people said to me, "Are you crazy? You got a restaurant, and you're gonna let them cater the food to them?" I said, "Ya, I'm not crazy. If they eat lunch here ever'day, there's gonna be people here lookin' for them." And that turned out great. We had *great* business!

The only thing about Ernest Borgnine is that you could *not* mess with him when he was eating lunch! He'd say, "No, I'm sorry, I'm eating lunch, I'm not talking to anybody. I'll answer your questions when I get through eating."

This movie was premiered in Fort Myers, so they got me a room in Fort Myers. I had to wear a tuxedo. In downtown Fort Myers, they blocked off a whole block. It was like Hollywood! I couldn't believe what happened. They built a stage on the street, they had a microphone and PA system, they had spotlights. They picked us up at the hotel in the limousine and when we drove up and got out of the limo, the spotlight was shining on us and everything. They announced who we were over the PA system. It was in all the Ft. Myers papers.

We watched the first showing of the movie. Then we went across the street to a big place where they had food and cocktails, and we just had a big party. That was thrilling.

Before the premier and all that, Paul, the guy who did the whole thing, wanted to come down and have a party at my place. So we arranged to have it all set up.

The name of the treasure hunter's boat in the movie was *The Lucky Lady*, and it had a buoy on it. The director was 6′7″, big son-of-a-gun! So they came down for this party, and, of course, I hadn't seen the movie yet. I was sitting at the bar, and this director came up to me and put his arm around me and I looked up at him.

The first thing I said to him was, "You son-of-a-gun! You cut me outta the movie, didn't ya?"

He said, "Now, now, wait a minute! You're still in there, but they did cut a little of it out, but you're still in there!" Then he said, "I brought you this buoy, I wanted to give it to you so you could hang it up in your chickee bar."

I knew then that they must have cut me! They cut out that line, where I was straight on at the bar. I don't know why they did, except maybe it wasn't necessary, maybe I didn't look good saying it, I don't know what it was. But the crowd liked it, I know that. Of course they just knew me, personally. So he gave me the buoy, and I've still got it.

Gone Fishin'

When a crew came down to film *Gone Fishin'* in this area, I was in the crowd scene.

They set up a fake pay phone out front. We were all sitting out in the parking lot like we were having lunch, and the one guy they're chasing is on the pay phone.

Whoever's in the car goes by and sees him, and he leaves right quick, gets in his car and goes the other way.

I just had to go down and see Willie Nelson in the Everglades, where he was in a scene. Jackie, the location gal who worked on *Captiva* which was done before *Gone Fishin'*, just loved our place, and she drank there every night. She was just a helluva gal.

She came over one night and told me about *Gone Fishin'*. She wanted me to come down and have lunch with her and the crew. I didn't want to do it because the cops and security people always try to tell you what you can and can't do on those sets. I told her I didn't want to go through all that.

But she told me she'd take care of that. So I went down there, and she did. We pulled in there, and that's when I ran into Joe Pesci and Danny Glover.

I pulled a good one on them too. They were standing there looking at me, and my girl friend, Lynn, who had on high heels and white short shorts. She was beautiful. We were walking towards them to go see Willie Nelson on the airboat behind them. When I got within talking distance of Joe and Danny, I don't know what made me say it, but I said, "Hey, you guys didn't never think I was this good, did ya?"

That Glover started laughing his ass off. I just figured they were looking at her. They gave me a big picture from the movie. I got it in the dining room.

Willie was doing a scene on the airboat, so I waited for him. When he finished, I told him about my birthday and his being the same and told him to come see us. This was Saturday, and he was supposed to come the next day. He didn't. I had the picture of him and me in the dining room. I had it all rolled up (it was taken on his bus about four years before that), and he signed it for me. He even put his phone number on it.

He said, "I'll come and see ya, but here's my phone number just in case somethin' happens."

I ended up calling him, and he couldn't make it. He had to get back to Nashville.

≈ 25 ≈

BENEFITS

We do a lot of benefits because I have the place to do it. I'm the type of guy who has helpfulness in his heart because of my background.

I was on welfare as a little kid till I was about 12 years old. And we were given stuff. I just want to give back, I guess. I feel like the good Lord put me in a place where I can do that. I'm so thankful that we're able to do that.

I do help out financially as well, but the biggest thing is just having a place to do it because the people who come, the people who give are the ones who really make it work.

The good Lord sent me the "Yankee Dollar" song, because I'm not a songwriter, they just come to me. I've taken in about $15,000 a year for charities with "Yankee Dollar," and I've been doing it for 18 years.

Shortly after we started our outside show 21 years ago, we got into doing benefits for people who needed our help. Of course, we always thanked God that we had the place to do this. We enjoy doing it. The tourists who come down get into it and really seem to enjoy it. They always contribute and make it work.

For a benefit, we get up on the stage and tell the people we're doing a benefit for whatever cause, and my good friends, Larry Scheetz and his wife, Kathy are very good helpers. They started helping me when we started doing Hospice eight or nine years ago. He's good at raffling off things, and she's good at getting people from her business, Accu-Care Nursing in Fort Myers and Naples, to help sell raffle tickets.

We do 50/50 money. We settled on every time we get $100, we'll give $50 away. Sometimes we'll elect to give 25/25 and have two winners. It just happens one way or the other.

I always sing that "Yankee Dollar" song for the yankee dollars, and they donate to whatever we tell them the cause is. That really works out good.

When I was doing Hospice benefits years ago, Jack Hamburger was so carried away with it because Hospice took care of his wife in her last days. Well, the next benefit we had for Hospice, he said to me, "Stan, don't sing the 'Yankee Dollar' song. Make it the 'Yankee One-*Hundred*-Dollar' song."

I said, "Why?"

He said, "I'll show you."

So when I did, he was so appreciative of the way they'd taken care of his wife that he came up and gave me five $100 bills. That was the *best* day ever singing the "Yankee Dollar" song. I've had several $100 bills given in the pot, but not five at one time!

In 2004 alone, we did benefits for the Asian tsunami disaster, hurricane damage support through Sunrise Rotary on Marco Island (Sarasota area), YMCA with Dottie Weiner, The Wishing Well Foundation (annually for the past four years), the American Cancer Society to benefit a lady motorcycle rider with with breast cancer, Hospice (annually), the Goodland Boat Parade (I've been the grand marshall for the past eight years; it ends up at my place; then they raffle off gifts and do 50/50s for Hospice of Naples), the Isles of Capri Fire Department (they wanted to buy a fast boat with a water tank on it so they could cover fires at sea), Father Pat—a priest on Marco—for the "Poorest of the Poor" kids in Peru and Haiti, Standing Watch (an organization against the opposition to building docks behind our houses on account of the manatees), and then we supported a little gal for student exchange to go to Spain from Lely High School.

We had a big benefit about two years ago when people were striking and walking picket lines against President Bush and the war in Iraq. I just felt like with our guys putting their lives on the line, that it just wasn't right to get out in the street and picket against them. I just couldn't see it.

We got support from the papers, and everyone who had been in the service wore their uniforms, and we had nurses there and Marines, Army, Navy, Air Force. We had all kinds of people. We took a lot of pictures and sent them up to Washington along with over 500 signatures stating that we were standing with our troops in that war.

Every time you turn around, we're benefitting somebody.

This puts me in mind of my brother, Floyd, who was four years younger than me. He didn't go to the service when Wally and I did because he was too young. So he was in high school all the time we were in the military.

Floyd weighed 160 pounds. Back in those days, kids weren't really *big*. If you had a guy who weighed 190 or 200 pounds, he was *huge*. We nicknamed Floyd "Butch" because he was tough, and he and I ran around together and fought together and had a helluva time.

He finished high school a year after we got back from the service. He was selected valedictorian of the senior class. Then he joined the National Guard unit right there in Bessemer.

When the Korean War came around, they pulled up the unit, and he had to join the Army. So he went in the Army, and 'course shortly after that, that war was over, no big deal with that.

But then he applied himself and put in for officer candidate school (OCS). With his background of being an "A" student and being the valedictorian, he got OCS and became a second lieutenant. He applied for the Air Corp, and they sent him to helicopter school at Ft. Rucker near Ozark, Alabama.

He graduated from that, and the Vietnam War came along. And where did he end up? He ended up in Vietnam. By then he'd made it to first lieutenant. He wanted to stay in, so he applied for regular Army, and was accepted.

They sent him to college in Omaha, Nebraska. He finished college in the service in Omaha. He then became a captain, and he made "Officer of the Day" and things like that at many of the bases he went to.

Finally, he ended up in Vietnam. They made him a lieutenant colonel, and he was in charge of a helicopter fighter squadron that fought at night with big search lights. They nullified everything on that San Pan River where the Vietcong were bringing supplies at night. They came up with the idea of the helicopters and the search lights and they actually killed everything that moved on that river, and they stopped all that.

Floyd ended up getting seven medals over there. He got everything but the Congressional Medal of Honor. He got the Flying Cross with the clusters, he got the Vietnam Country Award. He saved two black soldiers who were shot down in a field.

He also got shot down in Cambodia. Well, the bullets started about six inches behind his head, there were 30 bullet holes in the helicopter. But they sent one of those extra big helicopters over with the twin rotors and they lifted him up, helicopter and all, before the Vietcong got him.

So he had a pretty good life. After 24 years, he decided to hang it up. He could have gone on to be a full colonel, but he retired.

We had a big USO benefit party for the 50 years of the USO. We celebrated in Goodland at my place with an 18 piece orchestra in the Glen Miller mood. Everybody dressed in their uniforms. The late Betty Bruno got all this up with my okay, and we had the big party there on the stage and dancing. Oh, my God, it was a big party.

They knew about my brother, so she asked me if he would be the guest of honor, which he was, and he came in his dress whites with a gold braid. He came and he made the greatest speech you ever heard in your life. I'm so proud of him.

He was the only one of our whole family to finish high school, much less college. But he always gave my brother Wally and me credit for sending a military allotment back home to Bessemer so he could stay in school. That's what kept the house going, the money we sent back.

≈ 26 ≈

HEALTH PROBLEMS

I've had several times when my back would go out, like with muscle spasms or a pinched nerve—not a vertebrae or anything like that. I've found out with the experience I've had with back trouble that you have to absolutely nullify your body so your back will heal up. Of course, the doctors have ways of helping you do that, but it's a long process.

I've been to orthopedic doctors before, to chiropractors and everything. I've really not had any luck with the kind of problems I have with the muscles and the nerves. Sometimes cortisone shots help, sometimes they don't.

One time I had it real bad for *three months*. I'd been going to this orthopedic surgeon and he had X-rayed me, and every other thing like that. Then he put me on the cortisone pills for a week. Told me to call him back and I did.

He said, "Well, c'mon up here, but I don't know what I'm gonna do with you."

I thought that was kind of strange. Faye drove me up there. I couldn't sit down. I just could *not*. If I did, the pain was just unbelievable. So I draped myself over the back seat of the car and she drove me up there.

I went in his office, and it was full of people with broken legs and arms and whatever. They're all sitting down waiting, and I'm walking back and forth because I can't sit down! After about 30 minutes past my appointment, I decided, "I must be crazy! The guy said he didn't know what he was gonna do, and here I am in his office and I'm past my time by 30 minutes!"

So I went out to the car and Faye said, "Well, what'd he say?" I said, "I don't know, I didn't get to see him! Let's go to the pub and have some lunch, and go home, I guess."

So we went in there and I couldn't sit down in the dining room, and it was busy. People we looking at me and her and she said to me, "Can't you sit down?" I said, "No, I can't. I'll tell you what, you pay for lunch and I'm gonna go to the bar and get me a drink."

So I go in, stand up at the bar and asked for a double martini, and the guy that owns the place is Bill Smith and he says, "Damn, you still havin' trouble with that back?" I said, "Yup, this is three months now. I've been runnin' the business. I can walk down there, but I can't sit down, so I lay on my back in the store room with my feet on a chair, which they told me to keep my feet up, and it still hasn't relieved it."

About that time a little bread man came through there with a bunch of bread racks up on his shoulders, and Bill said, "Bread man, come here a minute. Tell this man what to do with his back!" He said, "You got to stay off your feet for about a week. Crawl wherever you go. You got to give it time to rest itself, to heal up."

Now it was between Christmas and New Year's, so we had some time off. I had Russ and his wife, Joanne, run the place. I took five days, stayed home, and started crawling around everywhere I went. The fifth morning I woke up, it was completely gone. I couldn't believe it—even to the point where I started talking to myself about it out loud: "You're gonna hurt. I know you are. You're not kidding me. You're gonna hurt, I know it!"

I'm still just trying to nullify my activities so my back will get better.

I've had it up and down before, even in Miami when I was working for the phone company stooping over and bending down to get under desks. I think that's what started it.

I couldn't get out from under a desk one day at a place in Miami. That was probablay 40 years ago. I was a young man, then. The chiropractor I was going to just kept fooling with me till finally I said, "I don't have enough money to keep doin' this!" He told me it would take care of itself if I just took it easy. Back then, it was $5 per treatment. I had no insurance either. So, sure enough, after a while, the pain subsided.

One time in my young life workin' for that phone company, they put me on an inside job. I was used to working outside, but they put me inside with a stressful job. I had to wear a headset and talk to several people on the headset, sometimes two or three at one time asking questions.

I also had to work with the frame guy down where the equipment was. It was an awful racket down there, like a freight train. They had a big speaker down there, and I could hear them yelling because I wasn't the only tester. There were about 12 of us.

This caused my stomach to start bothering me. It just made me nervous. So I went to the doctor, and he said, "Ya, you got the forerunner of an ulcer. You got a nervous stomach."

So he gave me this diet, and he said, "You can't drink, and you can't do this, and you can't do that," and all this stuff. So I'm putting up with that diet for about a week, and I'm just miserable, really.

My stomach was still bothering me. One night I came home from work irritable, and it was bothering me. I had a diet stuck up on the refrigerator so I could see it, and I said to my wife, "Faye, you know what? This stomach is botherin' me and I gotta get over it! How 'bout if I go down to the Post Inn (which was close to us by the Hialeah Race Track) and get a bottle of bourbon and let's have a drink."

"Well," she said, "you're not s'posed to drink."

I said, "I don't care, I'm sick of this diet, and it ain't helpin'."

So we came back and started drinking bourbon, and I looked up and saw that diet on the fridge. I went over there and tore it off, threw it in the trash can, and said, "I'm not lettin' anything bother me. I don't care what they do at that phone company, or how many of them yell and shout down there, I'm just gonna refuse to pay attention to it."

So I got over it. Mind over matter. Old Crow.

Anyway, that's some of the problems as you get older. People come up to me and say, "Oh, it's fun gettin' old ain't it?" Well, I really don't think about it that way. I always think about my wife passing at 47. She never even had a chance to get old. And here I am gettin' old and I don't know, I just feel blessed. I feel good about it.

And now I'm about to celebrate 80 years on this earth. We'll have a big party in Key West at Sloppy Joe's as usual.

≈ 27 ≈

REGRETS

I'm not a big shot. The things that happen in your life, that's just things that happen. It ain't no big deal. I don't like to look at life like a big deal because in the end you're going down and you ain't taking nothing with you. You ain't never seen a U-Haul following a hearse. So what's the big deal? Be happy that some of these things happen to you. That's okay, but to think you're a hot dude on account of it, no, I don't go for that.

I have no regrets for all the things my family's been through with going into debt and all the mortgages because I was absolutely *dedicated* to making the thing work—or die trying.

I've always worked hard, and I always believed in working hard for the man that hired me, and I still do feel that way. My prayers were answered when God put me over here in Goodland because Herb Robinson wouldn't sell the place to anybody but me! *He would not do it!*

So, I have no regrets about moving and bringing my wife over here and having three little kids sleeping in one room in a motel for eight months. Of course she didn't like it very much. She cried about it.

I have no regrets of the way I've lived my life. I've tried to treat everybody honest, and I believe in honesty. I know that's a hard word to live up to. I know I've slipped there too, but mostly that's the first thing I think about is being honest with whoever I'm dealing with.

I have no regrets of living this life that I've lived and am living.

Like the guy said, "Have you lived here all your life?" and the guy says, "No, not yet!"

I paid all my debts. Hospital bills, doctor bills when Faye was sick with cancer with no insurance. I don't mean to be bragging on myself, but I think it's very honorable when a man trusts you and helps you and loans you money or whatever. You're obligated to make it come back to him. I've always thanked God that I've got that in me. I get that from my mother, because she was that way.

I've been blessed. I always knew that God was on my side when I was working hard and trying to make those bills. I really don't think I ever worried about whether or not I was going to make it or not. (I hate that saying, "make it." What in the hell you gonna make? We all goin' outta here, *that's* what we're gonna make. We're all dyin'.)

I guess the only real regret I have is that I just didn't get an education. Some people I've said that to, said, "Well maybe that's a good thing. It might have ruined your personality!" (I say that loosely!) I never finished high school, but then I went ahead and tried to make something out of my life.

You can do that in America, *if* you set your mind to it. In America you can go as high as you want to go or as low as you want to go. It's your choice.

I just have no regrets for the way I've treated people, and I've met some great ones, like Lexie Herron my carpenter and good, good friend.

Gene Christian, a businessman in Ohio, helped me every way he could to make good decisions. He'd always talk to me, "Stan, are you doin' this?" I was always the type to ask people their opinions.

My wife would get me off to the side and ask, "Why do you ask these guys what their opinion is about things around here?" I said, "Because I wanna know what they think, and I'm not too smart, and when they give me their answer, I can decipher it with my thinkin' and what we're doin' here and get somethin' out of it. That's why I do that."

And it worked good for me, because a lot of people helped me along the way—*really* helped me along the way.

Al Repstorf of the First Bank of Marco Island was a lot of help to me. I'd get in a bind, I'd give him a call, he'd say, "Well, come over here and let's just do it." He was always very helpful. He ate with us, he brought people to eat with us, he was one of our "rooters." He *wanted* us to make it. He was a great guy in my life.

The only thing bad that ever happened to us was losing my wife. There's just nothing you can do about that. It was just one of those unfortunate things. But I got cards and letters—and I mean *boxes* full of them. Some guy drew a pencil drawing of me on the stage and wrote, "Thank you for all your good works, Stan, thank you."

That's gratifying when people come up to you and say, "thank you" for what you do.

I'm *so* happy that my kids and my family, myself included, never got on drugs. All during the drug days here, even though we were surrounded by drugs, we stayed clean. I'm proud of that.

My advice to young people would be, whatever you do, don't do drugs, because drugs will take over your mind, and you won't even know what's happening to you. And it's like they say, as you grow up, you probably will try a cocktail here and there, but the saying is, "If you get ahold of something you can't handle turn it loose!" If you can't handle alcohol, turn it loose, 'cause you can live without it.

I'd also like to advise you kids to get yourselves an education. Also, always honor your mother and father. That's the way it's got to be.

Another thing is, if you can find your way, find yourself a personal relationship with God because He's what will direct your life and guide you through your life. You're going to hit some bad spots in your life, and you're going to need some help other than a physical person on this earth. You're gonna have to reach out. So try to do that, and if you do that, you'll go through this life the best way you can.

The Bible says, "Love your neighbor as yourself." Help people who're less fortunate. That's our duty.

In our hometown, back in Bessemer, Alabama, the postmaster was a well-known, important job. Well, we lived in an old wooden house a block down from the postmaster, but they lived in a new house.

His boys and my brothers and I went to school together, so we played and everything, even though we didn't have *nothin'* and they had it all. They had the basement and the games and boxing gloves, football helmets, all the things a kid would want.

Every Sunday, their father, the postmaster, would take his kids and us swimming out to a place called Walnut Lake. He'd let us partake of the nice cabin they had in the woods and play with his kids and swim in that nice lake in the summer. And he'd bring us back to town and buy us ice cream sundaes.

That gets to me, y'know? He didn't have to do that. We didn't even have no nice clothes to wear. But he cared enough to do that. He was just loving his neighbor as himself. That's what he was doing.

Money ain't the answer. You can have all the money in the world, but when you go lay down to die, it won't help you.

It ain't the money. What's important is being like that postmaster in Bessemer. He did what he did because he had goodness in his heart. He probably wasn't expecting any special result. But probably because of him and because of my mom I've had goodness in my heart. And maybe I've been able to help people along the way. That's what's important.

Looking back on these 80 years I think if I had to do it all over again, I'd do it all over again.

And if you like this book and I live another 60 years we'll do a sequel.

Amen.

≈ 28 ≈

ASSORTED JOKES

I always could tell jokes. My aunt who lived with us growing up worked for the phone company, and she listened in on everybody in the world. Well, every time she heard a joke, she'd bring it home and tell us, and they just stuck with me.

Here's a few for you ...

Gotta Quit Smokin'

A guy goes to the doctor. The doctor checks him over, and the guy says, "Well, doc, whatta ya think?"

The doc says, "Well, you gotta quit that smokin', man."

So he changes doctors. The next doctor checks him over and says, "Feller, you gotta quit that smokin'!"

Well, the guy changes doctors *again*. The next doctor checks him over and says, "Well, you're okay."

The guy says, "Ain't you gonna tell me to quit smokin'?"

Doctor says, "Oh, no, man, it's too late for that now!"

Headache Remedy

A guy's talkin' to a fella 'bout havin' a bad headache. And the guy says, "Well, I'll tell you what, man, when I get a bad headache like that, I just go home and lay my head between my wife's breasts, and it soothes my headache. Maybe you ought to try that."

The guy says, "Well, I don't know what to do."

So he sees the guy about a week later, and he asks, "How's your headache, feller?"

He says, "It's gone!"

He says, "Did you do what I suggested?"

The guys says, "Yeah, man, you got a nice house too!"

Catholic Confession

Two Irish guys go down to the Catholic church. One of 'em says, "I gotta go confess. I committed adultery last week."

And his buddy says, "Well, go on in there and confess, man, and let's go out here and have some fun!"

So he goes in there and tells the priest that he committed adultery last week.

The priest says, "Well, who was it with?"

He says, "Oh, I can't tell you that."

And the priest says, "Was it Mrs. O'Shannesy?"

He says, "No."

"Was it Mrs. O'Neil?"

"No."

"Well, was it Mrs. O'Reilly?"

He says, "No." And he just gets all confused, so he gets up and walks out.

His friend says, "Did you confess?"

He says, "No, but I got us three good leads!"

The Golfer's Wife

Southwest Florida's pretty big in golf, and this guy goes to his wife and says, "Honey, we've been married over 40 years, and I was just wondering if you ever run around on me while I was playing golf?"

She says, "Well, maybe three times."

He says, "Three times?"

She says, "Well, that wasn't bad after all these years."

He says, "Well what was the first time?"

She says, "You remember when you had to have that operation when you had that little heart spell and you had to have a bypass and we didn't have the money? Well, I talked with the doctor, and he did that for us for nothin'."

Then she says, "Do you remember when we were talking about having the kitchen remodeled and we had termites and we didn't have the money? Well, I talked to this carpenter guy and he said that he could handle all of that for us. He did that for nothin'."

The husband says, "Oh."

Then she says, "Do you remember when you was runnin' for the county commissioner and you needed 60 votes to win? And you won?"

Boys' Brains

Then there was the lady giving her little boy a bath. As he was standing there nude, he looked down at himself and said, "Mama, are those my brains?"

She said, "No, honey, not yet."

Stranded Blondes

I tell a lot of blonde jokes. The one that I get a kick out of, because I watch the audience, and they look at me puzzled when I say this is,

"Did you hear about the two blondes that got stranded on the escalator when the power went off?"

The Old Couple and the Moon
(Dedicated to Neil Armstrong)

Neil Armstrong was headed to the moon. About that time there was a couple sittin' on the porch. It was an older couple listenin' to the music on the radio. So they were havin' a good time listenin' to that great old music back in those days. In a minute, the radio said, "*Newsbreak! Newsbreak! Newsbreak!* This is Walter Cronkite. Neil Armstrong is 4,000 feet from the moon!"

And with that her husband started laughing like crazy, and she looked at him puzzled. About that time the music came back on, and she didn't say anything.

A little while later, they're still listenin' to the music, and there it comes again, "*Newsbreak! Newsbreak! Newsbreak!* This is Walter Cronkite. Neil Armstrong has landed on the moon! We now have a man on the moon!"

And with that, her husband, the old codger, fell out of the chair laughin' and kickin' and rollin' around on the floor. And she looked down at him and said, "What in the world is wrong with you?!"

He said, "Well, Honey, you remember we got married 40 years ago, and I asked you for oral sex? You said, 'When there's a man on the moon!'"

The New Hat

There was another lady in her late 70s on a cruise ship. She went to the service store and bought herself a brand new nice panama-lookin' straw hat. She got right on the bow of the boat as it was movin' out to sea. The wind was blowing in, and she was about to lose her hat, so she put her hands up and was holdin' her hat on her head. When she did, her dress blew up.

A young man walked up to her and said, "Ma'am, you're exposing yourself."

She said, "Young man, what you're lookin' at down there is 70 years old, but this hat's brand new!"

A Dead Wife

Of course, there's the standard joke:

A guy says, "I think my wife's dead." And the other fella says, "Why?"

The guy says, "Well, the sex is the same, but the dishes are pilin' up."

Disappearing Wife

A cop stops this ol' feller, drivin' down the highway. So he says, "Whattsa matter, officer, did I do somethin' wrong?"

He says, "No, you didn't do anything *wrong*, I just wanted you to know that your wife fell outta the car back there about five miles!"

He says, "Oh, thank God! I thought I went deaf!"

Social Security

Y'know, there's a lot of talk about Social Security today. And so this old feller goes to his wife and says, "I'm gonna go down and get my Social Security before it's too late."

She says, "Aw, bologna, you can't get Social Security, you don't even have a birth certificate!"

He says, "Well, I'm gonna get my Social Security!"

So he goes down there for a while. When he comes back, she says, "Well, did you get it?"

He says, "Ya, I got my Social Security."

She says, "Well, how in the world did you do that without a birth certificate?"

He says, "I just took my hat off, showed the gray hairs on my head, then I ripped open my shirt, showed her the gray hairs on my chest, and she gave me my Social Security!"

She says, "Hmm. Well, while you was down there, why didn't you unzip your pants and let her look in there? You'd have got disability too!"

Deathbed Request

People sometimes send me jokes. A lady sent me this one:

One guy is on his deathbed and he says to his wife, "Honey would you please just give me one last request?"

She says, "Yes, yes darlin', anything!"

He says, "Will you marry Bob when I'm gone?"

She says, "Bob? I thought you hated Bob!"

He says, "I do."

The Ken Venturi Joke

This guy was making love to a woman in a hotel room. They had a great little session. He finished and picked up the hotel phone.

She said, "Who are you calling?"

He said, "I'm calling room service and getting us a bottle of champagne to celebrate our love making."

She says, "Oh but Ken Venturi wouldn't do that."

He says, "Why what would Ken Venturi do."

She says, "Ken Venturi would do ten pushups and then we would make love again."

So that's what the guy did. After making love again he picks up the phone to call room service.

She says, "Who are you calling now?"

He says, "I'm calling to get us a bottle of champagne to celebrate our love making twice

She says, "Ken Venturi wouldn't do that."

He says, "Well what would he do?"

She says, "He would take a shower and come back out here and do it again."

So that's what the guy did. Then as he picked up the phone and started dialing she says, "Who are you calling now?"

He says, "I'm calling Ken Venturi"

She says, "Why?"

He says, "I want to find out what par is on this hole."

Just a Minute

This guy went to talk to God one day, so he climbed a tall mountain. He got as high as he could and finally said, "God, I want to ask you something. What is a minute in heaven?"

God said, "A million years."

The guy said, "Well, what's a penny in heaven?"

And God said, "A million dollars."

So the guy said, "Well, God, will you loan me a penny?"

And God said, "Wait just a minute!"